VIDEO ETHNOGRAPHY

Video Ethnography describes how and why the audiovisual film medium is especially capable of transforming lived experience into vividly relatable forms of ethnographic knowledge. This essential text emphasizes the important role of the filmmaker, the variety of methods used in ethnographic films, and experiential ethics in order to describe how video ethnographies, in their production, are very closely bound up in the world of their subjects.

In this thought-provoking book, Redmon considers the complex ethics of video ethnography using case studies to show ethics in practice. The straightforward and concise approach of the text encourages students to craft their own video ethnographies with a fully conscious awareness of how certain skilled and attuned approaches to audiovisual techniques can help facilitate the fullest and most dynamic encounters possible. Redmon's unique approach effectively delves into theory, methods, and ethics, explaining how this kind of filmmaking can be a means of approximating, mediating, and evoking lived experience.

This book is suitable for undergraduate and postgraduate classes in ethnographic filmmaking, video ethnography, and visual anthropology/sociology.

David Redmon received his Ph.D. in sociology from SUNY-Albany. His documentaries have premiered at Sundance, Toronto, Museum of Modern Art, Viennale Film Festivals, and other international destinations. Redmon is a former Radcliffe Fellow and Film Studies Fellow at Harvard University. He is currently an independent scholar, filmmaker, and Fellow at the IMéRA Institute for Advanced Study at University of Aix-Marseille, France.

VIDEO ETHNOGRAPHY

Theory, Methods, and Ethics

David Redmon

Routledge
Taylor & Francis Group

LONDON AND NEW YORK

First published 2019
by Routledge
2 Park Square, Milton Park, Abingdon, Oxon OX14 4RN

and by Routledge
52 Vanderbilt Avenue, New York, NY 10017

Routledge is an imprint of the Taylor & Francis Group, an informa business

British Library Cataloguing-in-Publication Data
A catalogue record for this book is available from the British Library

Library of Congress Cataloging-in-Publication Data
A catalog record has been requested for this book

ISBN: 978-0-367-17352-4 (hbk)
ISBN: 978-0-367-17353-1 (pbk)
ISBN: 978-0-429-05632-1 (ebk)

Typeset in Bembo
by Swales & Willis, Exeter, Devon, UK

CONTENTS

ACKNOWLEDGEMENTS

Thanks to my parents for encouraging me to read as a young child. I wholeheartedly thank the Leverhulme Trust for awarding this project a research grant. This book, and the film *Sanctuary* cited in it, would not have been possible without your support. I also wish to acknowledge the Radcliffe Institute for Advanced Study at Harvard University for providing a summer Radcliffe Fellowship in the heart of Cambridge where the Sensory Ethnography Lab was born. I would like to provide special thanks to Boris Petric for awarding a Fellowship at *La Fabrique* in Marseille, France. Your patience and kind support helped me push through the difficulties of completing this project. Thank you Mike Martinez, my students, and especially my loving family Ashley, Magnolia, and Matteo. Thank you Deborah and Dale for your endless friendship and support to help make this book – and movies – possible. Finally, thanks to Joanna Rabiger for your reading and assistance in editing this manuscript.

INTRODUCTION

I began writing this book from beyond the walls of academic institutions or academic employers, as what one might call a "feral" ethnographer, having deliberately strayed from the world of education to make my own documentary films – films that are steeped in ethnographic sensibilities yet not, in any academic or scholarly sense, formally speaking, ethnographic. When I made these films I was operating from far beyond the world of teaching, or learning from students. I had no administrative duties or departmental meetings to pursue. I was free to make documentaries any way I wanted, in ways that drew on lived experience yet weren't constrained by disciplinary restrictions. I was able to follow my own instincts about my approach to documenting various worlds, subcultures, and subject matter, and I was able to develop my own working methodology and theory of what I was doing and why it was significant.

The films I made during this time seemed far too personal, unrestricted, unsupervised, and "wild," to constitute actual, sound, legitimate academic knowledge. Yet, nearly a decade later, academic institutions are beginning to accept and show interest in the kind of work I, and others, were conducting on their own, beyond institutionality. In the past decade, various departments within academic institutions have begun adopting what is generally called "video ethnography" and, as a result, a new wave of teaching and practice-related institutional theorizing has begun gathering force. The documentary genre has also exploded in popularity, in the wider public world, in the past decade. Academia reflects this new popularity and also helps shape it. Modules and classes on video ethnography have increased; a few journals are starting to publish online digital documentaries and film festivals are becoming spaces to disseminate ethnographic documentaries as public knowledge, up for discussion, through panels and at conferences of all kinds, including social work, critical military studies, and other disciplinary and vocational areas of academia.

In this new age of the rise of documentary film, with more and more documentaries streaming online and commanding vast audiences on television and in cinemas in theatrical release, with reviews, social media commentary, and Q&As at film festivals proliferating, and as public discussion of documentary films increases, the time is ripe for academia to catch up and to apply academic rigor and exploration of documentary films, not merely as finished products, but in terms of their making, craft and impulse. Film festivals and documentary organizations have long debated the ethics and methodology of documentary film. In the past some of these films reached only small audiences, and remained within a relatively closed culture of documentary filmmakers and narrow audiences. Today, as documentary films that can be broadly called "video ethnography" circulate widely, attracting diverse and nonspecialist public attention, I believe it is more important than ever for academia to look closely at the authorial, exploratory, and expressive intentions behind process and craft, aspects of ethnographic film that have traditionally been more closely studied within film studies and as part of film production courses. For example, the editing decisions filmmakers make to construct their documentaries or ethnographies, and the outcomes of distributing such films into the public sphere – something that filmmaker, film critic, and scholar David MacDougall has indicated in *Transcultural Cinema* (1998) and *The Corporeal Image* (2006) – have been omitted in ethnographic film studies.

In *Transcultural Cinema*, MacDougall (1998, p. 1) shares the following statement, about the need to write about his filmmaking process – a statement that struck a deep chord, as I began exploring my own questions while writing this book:

> Much of this writing was done as a kind of counterweight to the experiences of filmmaking, for making films generates countless questions that films themselves can only address indirectly … Still other [questions] I have struggled for years in filmmaking but that may finally be unanswerable. In addressing them I share Dai Vaughan's belief that it is important to make the effort, even if one arrives at only an incomplete understanding … These essays sometimes have a similar purpose, in seeing whether certain things can be put into words. They also borrow from my belief that filmmaking should be a process of exploration, rather than a way of stating what you already know.

I feel an affinity with MacDougall's carefully chosen words – especially in his emphasis on filmmaking as a process of exploration, a key idea that I will explore extensively in this book.

Video ethnography

"Video ethnography" is a cinematic approach to recording ethnographic expressions of lived experiences. There are many other ways of evoking lived experience using other mediums: for example, sound design, painting, musical composition, choreography, and more. In *Video Ethnography* I am wholly focused on the cinematic approach. In this book I seek to describe how and why the audiovisual film medium is especially capable of transforming lived experience into vividly relatable forms of ethnographic knowledge. One of the key facets of the medium lies in its technology, but in this book I will repeatedly emphasize the important role of the body of the filmmaker, the varying methods, and experiential ethics in order to describe how video ethnographies, in their production, are very closely bound up in the world of their subjects (Grimshaw and Ravetz 2009).

One of the most striking features of filmmaking is that it uses precise technology to share the experiential life of animals, objects, environments, and people within a haptic, acoustic, and visual aesthetic. Video ethnography is capable of bringing audiences into the world of the subject in striking, visceral ways. Its starting point is an embodied encounter in which the filmmaker inhabits the same space as his or her subject, be it a static landscape, a mobile animal, or human being, in any setting – from office space to field of labor or inside a home (Buescher and Urry 2009; Garrett 2011). It could even be the world of an insect, or a fish, deep underwater. Sharing such intimate space over the duration of time raises methodological and ethical questions that I will also explore. This intimacy and sharing of worlds that occurs in the creation of video ethnographies is key to the dynamic encounter between filmmaker and subject, and in this book I will seek to ground the characteristics and shaping forces of the video ethnographic approach within methodological and ethical rigor. In some sense this book is my response to David MacDougall's call for the need to write and think deeply about filmmaking itself, not only the films produced, and his emphasis on filmmaking as exploration that I referred to above, in a citation from his book *Transcultural Cinema*.

Video ethnography is a recent movement within the social sciences that has emerged out of more-than-representational theory (Vannini 2016), meaning that it offers more than simply an aesthetic representation because it is capable of exploring subjects and "worlds" in knowledge-producing ways, for example, as a process of creation and evocation of societal, cultural, and individual knowledge study, as a form of research (visual note-taking) within the fields of visual anthropology, visual sociology, and cultural studies (Cubero 2009, 2015). In this book I seek to show how video ethnography is inherently an exploratory and relational experience by using visual and acoustic sensory knowledge as a mode of attuned, tentative inquiry through which to explore and evoke the complexity of social life. Video ethnography plunges into lived experience and offers a bodily, visual, and sonic mode of *evocation* of subjects and their worlds, expanding the available means of knowledge production beyond the written text or written description. Unlike a textual analysis of lived experience, it breaks with the conventions of academic publishing in which the written word dominates, and also provides sensuous evidence of the researcher's recording conditions and circumstances. For example, filming subjects in heavy rain conveys the experiences that heavy rain produces, from the auditory experience of how sound changes when it rains, to slick conditions underfoot, how subjects embody and move in the atmosphere, and so on, in ways that would be difficult to achieve in the written medium. In this way, video ethnography tends to feel more participatory, or present, with its subjects and their environment than textual analysis, because of the visceral immediacy of the medium. Furthermore, unlike textual analysis, video and sound complicates this relationship so that instead of observing the subject through the written word, we, as viewers and listeners, tend to inhabit the same space as the subjects, much as the filmmaker did, and are placed in a more empirical mode of understanding (Pink 2009; Simpson 2011).

There is a 20th century tendency in visual sociology to interpret and study pre-existing images or sounds from two primary frameworks: (1) a social scientific paradigm of collecting premade images as "data" and (2) a cultural studies paradigm of semiotics that desperately attempts to extract and impose pre-existing meaning onto images and sounds. Neither approach requires us to think about or explore the filmmaker/researcher's participatory presence or involvement with the people, animals, or objects presented in the images. Within these paradigms, the actual work and physical labor of producing images and sounds has been done by others, while it is the job of the researcher to sit and analyze the meaning of the image or sound by inscribing an ideological or conceptual tag to them. The exploration of the filmmaker's role in capturing, sharing, and shaping lived experience is excised.

Video ethnography, in contrast to the two approaches summarized above, favours the production of phenomenological and more-than-representational inquiries into sensuous life as a distinct way of knowing, relating and understanding – it requires the researcher's presence as he or she records lived experience. Video ethnography is in opposition to textual sociology's emphasis of utilizing written words to make and interpret meaning, as if "meaning" is somehow prior to how lived experience is experienced. By challenging the practice of semiotic research and its researchers, who attach meaning to images and sounds in a mode of analytical study and analysis, video ethnography is intellectually invigorating, turning away from retrospective meaning-making and instead crafting, and inflecting the sumptuousness, or vivid intricacy and complexity, of sensuous life.

By differing so significantly from semiotics, video ethnography very much answers Vannini's (2015a) call for more researchers to find a way to go beyond representational literalism. Whereas representation attempts to create an accurate portrait of its subjects of study (Vannini 2015b), a more-than-representational approach to ethnographic research attempts to

> animate rather than simply mimic, to rupture rather than merely account, to evoke rather than just report, and to reverberate instead of more modestly resonating, in this sense offering a true escape from the established academic habit of striving to uncover meanings and values that apparently await our discovery, interpretation, judgment and ultimate representation.
>
> *Lorimer 2005, p. 84 cited in Vannini 2015a, p. 318*

Vannini (2014a, p. 3) contends that "video methods are less useful for capturing reality than they are for evoking distinct, multiple, competing, and often contradictory aural and visual impressions." The advantages of video ethnography do not lie in its ability to replicate the human eye, but in that it doesn't even attempt to do this and therefore allows us to "see [and hear] the world differently from our habitual ways of looking and feeling" (Vannini 2014a, pp. 391–416).

Vannini suggests there is nothing that can be physically captured by a camera or by written word, or indeed by any other means of representation. The camera can be deployed as part of a sensibility intended to produce an experience for viewers distinct from simply being there, using one's human senses. The camera encourages viewers to see, hear, feel, and interpret an environment in a completely different way because of its technology, thus enhancing sensory knowledge beyond that which could be gained from experiencing a situation with the eyes, ears, and bodies. This approach endeavors to generate a sense of meaning, not derived from reflecting on an experience but instead evoked by sensory experience (Vannini 2015a). Its

> orientation to the temporality of knowledge, for [more-than]-representationalists are much less interested in representing an empirical reality that has taken place *before* the act of representation than they are in enacting multiple and diverse potentials of what knowledge can become *afterwards*.
>
> *Vannini 2015a, p. 12b*

This methodology generates audiovisual sensory experiences to elicit impressions in viewers that extend beyond the range and impact of written communication (Lorimer 2010; Vannini 2014b). The ability of ethnographic videography to evoke lived sensory experience for viewers is the central tenet and the basis for the methodological style of case study featured in this book.

Vannini's (2012, 2015a) success in integrating video ethnography with more-than-representational theory has resulted in the evolution of a dynamic ethnographic sensibility (Vannini 2015a) that encourages researchers to immerse themselves in the sensuous world of their subjects and their environments, in order to be able to fully evoke their lived textures. Traditional text-based ethnography is

> largely a discourse of written words, but how often in talking with another researcher, has the conversation moved from data and analysis into the field experience: the heat, the smell, the press of people, the subtlety of a gesture, the bleakness of the landscape, the quiet in the garden, or the hallucinatory overload of a festival?
>
> *Bishop and Bishop 2013, p. 132*

An increasing number of ethnographers have begun to consider elements of the social world that cannot be rendered adequately in research confined to written analysis alone (Vannini 2015a). Such an approach requires researchers to get their hands and feet dirty and to plunge themselves into lived experiences.

Building on my previous work in ethnographic filmmaking, I have begun writing about the experiential approach to crafting non-fiction cinema to mark the arrival of a new approach in the social sciences that conveys and produces sensuous knowledge as media (Rose 2007). Researchers have been reluctant to integrate technologies such as sound recorders, editing software, and digital video cameras to record and transfigure lived experiences into sensory scholarship. Anthropology, by contrast, has a long, robust history of merging the above technologies to produce ethnographic movies. The Sensory Ethnography Lab (SEL), founded by Lucien Castaing-Taylor at Harvard University, is perhaps the best known contemporary example of scholarship to go beyond words, text, and image. Castaing-Taylor and colleagues at the SEL have produced a wide range of ethnographic media works such as sound recordings, installations, documentaries, and mixed media that invite audiences into atmospheres of color, space, sound, and landscapes of experience. These scholastic works of radical empiricism deliver immersion and affective relationships rather than argumentative or expository prose to provide a sense of being there.

"Sensory Ethnography" of this kind elicits sensuous responses in viewers; changing breath patterns, causing the skin to tingle, moving the emotions, involving sight and perception, and expanding the ability to hear and feel a soundscape through one's body. Text, by contrast, flattens the plentitude and complexity of lived experience and collapses its wildness into left-to-right textual representation intended to be read chronologically and in order. Indeed, reflecting on the strengths of a multisensory approach to creating experiential scholarship brings to light a more general crisis for representation in the social sciences (Vannini 2015a). Ethnographic filmmaking contributes a new form of methodological sensibility through which to attend to more than is possible by the medium of text alone. Together, these modes of conveying lived experiences are capable of expansive complexity, or what Merleau-Ponty (2012) calls "brute" or "wild experience." A text combining images, sound, and motion can elicit synesthesia in viewers by inviting immersion in expansive complexity – the ability to mediate the complexity of lived experience that is generally missing from representational text. This kind of focus on mediating raw experience is transforming the social sciences and has opened up a range of exciting new possibilities to cross-fertilize and disseminate multisensory scholarship.

I believe that it is now time to move forward from the social sciences' staple-of-the-discipline role of interpreting film, art, sound, and photography, to actually producing and making films and reflecting more upon that experience as a means of understanding the world and knowledge production. I would like to see the social sciences create sound recordings alongside scholarly textual interpretations, explanations, and findings; and to explore the social world through literature, including poetry and fiction. In this book I seek to foster a practice-based approach to the work of evoking lived experience.

I also seek to explore the embodied nature of filmmaking, to explore how video ethnography is inherently reflexive, acknowledging how a filmmaker's/ researcher's presence alters filmed situations and how the filmmaker is also transformed by filming situations. I can do this best through case studies, especially through reference to my own experience of making films.

Cultivating a thoughtful practice-based approach to knowledge production and fostering more discussion of decisions made during production, and thoughts about them, is one of the central aims of this book. Referring to his sensory ethnography documentary *Demolition* Sniadecki (2014, p. 29) writes

> My decision to refrain from allowing spoken language and text a primary position in the first quarter of the film derives from my awareness that both speech and text possess the power to detract from viewers' ability to attend to more experiential and sensorial aspects, colonizing the image and soundtrack. Yet through a balance of the verbal and nonverbal, the representation of humans as speaking subjects – which is most often privileged in nonfiction filmmaking – does not overwhelm the representation of humans as sensual, emotional, and material beings. In short, my goal was for these modes of human experience to receive relatively equal treatment in the film.

These kinds of thoughtful reflections about filmmaking amply demonstrate the embodied and reflexive relationship of the filmmaker. In this instance, the filmmaker attunes to the idea of nonverbal lived experience and carefully considers how to mediate his encounters with his subjects to viewers as a form of expressive contact that goes beyond mere recording.

The kind of methodological framework based in observation and thoughtfulness that Sniadecki describes above forms a key part of my emphasis on the importance of what I call "learning to attend" when making video ethnographies. Learning to attend demands more of us than the critical, analytical position of semiotic and textual analysis. It is a facet of production itself, rather than analysis. Learning to attend takes us into the presence of, and into deep observational involvement with, subjects, to produce an expressive form of knowledge that is sensitive to subjects, environment, and to the choice-making aspects of filmmaking, including postproduction choices. Learning to attend is a process of asking questions of oneself: how can I best attend to the object of my attention – animal, or human, or landscape, or other environment? Is it necessary to move, or remain immobile or stationary, to attune? Video ethnography as a practice involves asking oneself questions while filming and later in postproduction that epistemologically position us, as filmmakers, in close relation to the lived flux of sensations and encounters that are part of all social activities (human, animal, etc.). Attending to our shared affective fabric – the materiality of existence – brings with it an experiential approach to sensorial meaning-making. It's this active, exploratory, questioning approach inherently demanded by video ethnography as a practice that I seek to share and discuss, through case studies, including my own films.

It remains relatively rare to hear about or discuss the conditions under which video ethnographies are made and how these conditions factor into the production of cinematic knowledge and understanding. Video ethnography involves sharing the same space and world as the subject and remaining in sensuous contact with subjects and their worlds. It is inherently immersive and experiential. Video ethnographers are often mobile in their approach, flowing with and brushing up against the shared dynamics of the situation, quite literally thinking on their feet. Video ethnographers often accept chance, unknown encounters, and drift as part of the skilled sensibility of cinematic movement.

Along with rapidly following changing dynamics, filmmakers making video ethnographies become skilled at maintaining encounters with subjects that are not fixed in place by an interview setup or by a more formal approach. This approach can entail following subjects under challenging circumstances – ethical, dangerous, and/or intimate encounters. Throughout this process, filmmakers must practice skilled attunement in order to stay focused on their subjects, or, in other words, keep the camera running through thick and thin and continue moving with the subject. This skill means that video ethnographers are able to mediate lived experience whole and on the fly, without cuts or edits, pauses or distraction, deepening the time spent in the environment for the viewer so that viewers become immersed in the same environment in which the filmmaker was himself or herself situated while running the camera. An outcome of this approach is what can be called extended duration. Extended duration can be a choice, on the part of filmmakers, to keep intact, or whole, or relatively uninterrupted in the final film, through editing choices made in postproduction, long durations of immersive film. The implications for video ethnography of long stretches of uninterrupted filming are radical. Extended duration allows audiences to more fully absorb and understand the logic, meaning, and continuity of embodied and mobile experiences.

Producing video ethnography using the skills that allow for extended duration permits the filmmaker as a researcher to become deeply involved in and immersed with the more-than-representational qualities of lived experience and to widely share this living fabric with audiences. Such an approach requires the skill to blend in or merge with the world or environment being filmed, and to finesse the practice of observation. Experiential encounters are not just raw, uncut episodes. They require the filmmaker's judgement and are balanced with skills of decision-making and interpretation. As important as movement is to attunement, the ability to choose to stay still is equally important. The researcher-as-video ethnographer moves the camera and sound recorder to direct attention to people, animals, and/or objects through skilled, thoughtful attentiveness. Observation always occurs from somewhere, or a point of view, and this somewhere, or point of view, requires the skill of attention and the ability to direct attention to crucial textures of lived experiences that form part of everyday life.

Despite my decision to explore this topic through written language, I won't pretend that my words can fully, partially, or even minimally translate audiovisual experiences into sensuous encounters – they can't. Likewise, I do not pretend to speak or write for any of the ethnographic films addressed in this book, or the people who made them. I recognize the limitations of words, which can never provide a substitute for experience. As Lucien Castaing-Taylor and Véréna Paravel suggest, such projects are irreducible:

> We're human beings so we're constantly interpreting. The problem is that most of the time when we're interpreting ourselves and our actions and other people, trying to give some meaning to life, we're doing it in a very inconclusive way. An interpretation that we come to now would be different from one we come to in six months' time. Interpretations mutate as we go through life and have different experiences, so the moment a filmmaker assigns one to a film it constrains the aesthetic potentialities that the film can put into play.[1]

Likewise, I accept that, in the textual medium, my analysis will inevitably reduce video ethnographies to mere words on a page. Nevertheless accepting that, even within these limitations, I believe it is still important to discuss the characteristics and capabilities of video ethnographies and the components of its practice, and I seek to cultivate more such conversations through sharing my thoughts in this book.

Lived experience

Video ethnography is concerned with mediating the lived experience of people, animals, objects, and places immersively, rather than situating subjects within a discursive, overtly informational frame. This approach requires audiences to attend to lived experience without relying on voice-over, or verbal explanation, or other forms of exposition, for example, without relying on interviews that explain what they are watching. Making video ethnographies is a conscious choice to show experience rather than to explain or "tell" it, or refer to it with words. The video ethnographer tends to preserve sensuousness or somatic qualities in the lived experience mediated through film, as a form of knowledge and understanding.

The somatic, or bodily, aspects of video ethnography and its tendency to observe or show rather than tell are far-reaching and mark a break with other forms of conveying ethnographies. First, lived or somatic experience precedes consciousness, language, and symbolism in precognitive ways. It entangles and wraps bodies together through synesthetic encounters. The body sees sounds, hears textures, tastes colors, or smells touch. Visceral experiences of synesthesia arise from the embodied relationship of the filmmaker to the world they are filming. As they film, the camera becomes an extension of the human body. The body guides the camera to listen to sounds, to perceive interactions, and to carefully and thoughtfully move in unplanned, flowing ways within the rhythms of the routine of an environment, or habitat. Observed closely over time, camerawork of this kind is seen to dance, hum, and even sing. Attending to the synesthetic circumstances of lived experience using audiovisual technology allows video ethnographers to focus on how "raw" expression takes place through the senses, prior to semiotic or cultural significations. The result is a highly attuned, vital mediation of lived experience that is alive to gesture and flux.

Producing experiential knowledge through audiovisual means

My personal approach to the practice of video ethnography lies somewhere between observational, participatory, and immersive ethnography. In graduate school, empirical studies shaped my training but it was audiovisual work that really captivated me. Early in my studies, I learned how to practice the skills of a *written* ethnographer, and later, while defending my dissertation, I presented audiovisual recordings of lived experiences to accompany my written work. After my Ph.D., I taught myself how to use audiovisual devices to shape lived experiences into "dramatic" ethnographic stories with plots, characters, tension, and conflict. However, like most stories in motion, something happened along the way that redirected my focus on narrative: I encountered Lucien Castaing-Taylor and colleagues such as David MacDougall at the SEL. It was their approach that led me to move away from the need to produce a forced *narrative* trope with conflict and resolution.

When I first came across the SEL filmmakers and witnessed how they produced films about lived experience in non-narrative, open-ended formats, I experienced a range of contradictory emotions: I was thrilled and sad, I felt empty and yet also restored, silenced and exuberant. I felt both clarity and confusion. As an engaged ethnographer, why hadn't I come across this particular approach earlier? After all, I had committed myself to voraciously watching as many non-fiction and fiction movies as possible. After watching Castaing-Taylor and Barbash's documentary *Sweetgrass*, I felt as though I had encountered several nuanced ways to approach and create non-fiction. I reproached myself for wasting ten years shaping lived experiences into story-orientated narratives, and I began to question the benefits of a narrative approach to storytelling.

Why, for instance, did I assume it was necessary to impose an artificial closure on a story riddled with contradictions and messy in its arbitrary ending? Why did I include non-diegetic music? Why did I think it was important to remove confusion and to add clarity, or what is often called "signposting" to a story? "If life is messy and unpredictable, and documentary is a reflection of life, should it not be digressive and open-ended too?" were words written in Castaing-Taylor's

Image/Sound/Culture syllabus – the outline for his pedagogical practice of sensory ethnography.[2] Encountering this sensibility opened up for me an unforeseen space from which I felt much freer to adopt fluid approaches to conveying lived experiences. It was a license to dare, and it provided a liberating opportunity to experientially experiment with long takes of duration without the use of montage, allowing me the promise of exploring lived experience without a reliance on spoken words or prose.

Language, text, and words

VÉRÉNA PARAVEL: And this is the problem. Every time we talk about the film [Leviathan] we're trying to make sense of it through our prose, but then when I'm at all these screenings, watching the first 20 minutes to check the sound, what I'm seeing has nothing to do with all the bullshit that comes out of our mouths. We're trying desperately to put some words to it and we're attached to this thing, but every time I'm sitting there I think this is absolutely bullshit. This film is way, way beyond our words. It sounds super pretentious to say that.

LUCIEN CASTAING-TAYLOR: But it happens to be true.[3]

The above excerpt, taken from an extensive conversation between the ethnographic filmmakers Lucien Castaing-Taylor and Véréna Paravel and film critic Jason Ward[4] raises a few important questions that highlight a divide between video ethnography and written or textual ethnography. How is it possible to attach words to lived experiences and into a linear narrative when it resists encapsulation by the reductive capacities of language? How can words written in this book serve to interpret a film like *Leviathan*, when the film's directors themselves refuse to use written or spoken language as a way of making sense of it? Again, I quote Castaing-Taylor:

We're much more than linguifying creatures. In fact, when we're born, we're imaging creatures, we're sounding creatures, we're tactile creatures, we're these haptic, somatic, physical bodies and minds all working together in some inextricable way. And so to reduce representations of the world to those which can be rendered in academic, sentential, propositional prose seems to be incredibly limiting. So we're trying to use media to … present human and animal existence in a way that's not usually done either in the art world, in documentary, or in the academy.[5]

One of the many problems with using words is their slipperiness. Words are associative, embedded in a network of conscious and unconscious associations, across different languages and histories. Words struggle to stand in for complete, or even partial, experience, because they reside exclusively inside the realm of the semiotic or symbolic communication. At most, language can provide us with metaphors to describe the real. To minimally grasp the real, one must also touch, taste, smell, see, and/or hear it. In short, the real is sensed; it is experienced, felt, tasted, licked, smelt, heard, and touched by corporeal bodies. Yet, I contend along with David MacDougall, there must be an attempt to write about or aim at the real, too. In an extremely clear paragraph worth quoting at length, David MacDougall explains ethnographic filmmakers' need for words:

> ethnographic filmmakers, possibly even more than others, tend to write little about their work, perhaps believing that in the academic world this can only result in superficiality – a substitution of words for the products of their labor. They may even take a perverse pleasure in foiling this process. "Making a film," says Jean Rouch (1985) "is such a personal thing for me that the only implicit techniques are the very techniques of cinematography ... It is also very difficult for me to talk about it and, above all, write about it." Filmmaking also consumes more energy than is generally apparent to outsiders, often leaving little room for writing. Moreover, it entails a fundamentally different attitude toward communicating with others. Rouch has made over a hundred films, but produced only a handful of articles about film itself. Similar explanations could be given for the relative silence of other figures in ethnographic film, such as Robert Flaherty, John Marshall, Timothy Ash, and Ian Dunlop. It is not that filmmakers are unreflective, for they are often quite talkative about their work, but the ideas, descriptions, and reflections they express are ephemeral. This is the perspective most easily lost to history. What survives in writing is usually fragmented and anecdotal. If we had them, more comprehensive, fine-grained accounts of the filmmaking process would allow us to compare our own ideas of films with an understanding of how the filmmaker's ideas and desires had been pursued in them, within the intellectual and artistic movements of their times. They would allow us to see how a film had progressed through the phases of planning, production, and editing and to witness the filmmaker's struggles to define issues, confront epistemological problems, and make his or her ideas and understanding manifest. Ideally, such an account would interrogate the filmmaker and the work at every stage of its production, although in most cases this is probably impractical. But until we have more full-length accounts by filmmakers, we will have to settle for less exhaustive testimony – diaries, production notes, interviews, and recorded conversations.
>
> *Barbash and Castaing-Taylor 2007, pp. 32 and 153–154*
> *citing Robert Gardner*

In this book I want to echo and also act on David MacDougall's concern that few filmmakers in the social sciences and humanities write about their films. To address the problem of a lack of written material by ethnographers who practice filmmaking, this book assembles personal interviews, written statements, audio interviews, production notes, DVD commentaries, and videorecorded conversations with contemporary people who make video ethnographies such as Lucien Castaing-Taylor, J.P. Sniadecki, Véréna Paravel, Ilisa Barbash, and Ernst Karel. It also includes filmmakers's written statements about their movies, the process of making them, and their conceptual approaches to mediating lived experience using film.

The social sciences and humanities, now more than ever, need diverse approaches, including the written approach, to pushing experiential film ethnographies into interdisciplinary spheres of production. This leads me to pose a question: what would multidisciplinary or interdisciplinary video ethnography projects actually look, sound, and affectively feel like? What would be their tactile, synesthetic, and sonorous qualities? The scope, magnitude, and development of an actual audiovisual epistemology committed to mediating all the complexity of lived experiences seems so enormous that even positing it as an option seems to border on the absurd. Yet, an experiential approach nevertheless offers several possibilities to introduce an even more absurd notion: forging a bridge between the practice of the arts in the humanities and the study of lived experiences in the social sciences.

Art and lived experience: aesthetics and digital media

While in the past the senses and sensuous immersion have not formed much part of the respectable academic realm of the social sciences and humanities, there has been recent growing interest in sensuousness and in the somatic as viable modes and mediums for deepening understanding and for legitimate academic knowledge building. Thanks to a range of initiatives and movements, such as Lucien Castaing-Taylor's development of the SEL and Phillip Vannini's Innovative Ethnography Series, as well as Boris Petric's initiation of La Fabrique, David Howes' Sensory Institute, and Erin Manning and Brian Massumi's Sense Lab, researchers today are more likely to incorporate somatic elements. The above-mentioned labs and initiatives, based in or around academic institutions, serve to foster an exuberant mix of ethnography, art, and performance, and help to shift the idea of knowledge production away from the discursive realm, and to legitimize expressive, aesthetic, and sensuously immersive projects as respected areas of research within the broader and more traditional academy.

These initiatives have emphasized how digital media is an increasingly significant tool for opening up researchers' opportunities to experiment with what would previously have been labeled "art," meaning that researchers have been able to make films. Through these films they have been able to explore lived experiences in visceral, immersive ways, even within academic disciplines that have more traditionally relied upon the written medium. Projects based in video ethnography are increasingly acceptable and even valued. In this book I argue that video ethnography as a research tool and medium is well suited to mediating the complexity of lived experience. This rich complexity is what makes it so valuable. Furthermore, the somatic or sensuous elements that such projects include, by using video ethnography, reveal that lived experience has an aesthetic component. By this I mean that we are sensing, seeing, hearing, feeling animals and we experience the physical world as a visual and acoustic environment, meaning that various aesthetic aspects are what give a sense of place and of concrete reality. For example, a film that takes place in a physical environment is more likely than a written essay or article to convey the aspects that vividly make up the environment – its colors, sources of lighting, sounds, and all fleeting perception. A film set in a particular space conveys these elements with immediacy, rather than relying on the symbolic domain of words or text, presenting them simultaneously. In this way the video ethnography creates a distinct epistemological space that allows media ethnographers to show, hear, and feel the aesthetic textures of sensuous life in practice. Through this epistemological space, ethnographers, and thus viewers or audiences, are able to investigate the atmosphere, vibrancy, and authenticity of places (Garrett and Hawkins 2014). For example, video ethnography might be used to explore a place such as a city market, an airport, a ferry, a restaurant, or a kitchen. Increasingly the advantages of video ethnography have become clear and it has gained acceptance within academia.

Nevertheless, there remains a lack of agreement or consensus about how video ethnographies can and should be made. I argue that there is a wide range of possible approaches to making video ethnographies and I assert that it is this very freedom of range and open-ended quality that gives video ethnography its value (Kusenbach 2003; Spinney 2015). Video ethnography has an inherently malleable aesthetic that leaves the researcher or practitioner free to explore all facets and dimensions, expressive and otherwise. I assert this amid a context of rule-bound, rule-making, and cautionary verbiage surrounding video ethnography. Currently, most books on ethnographic film are instructional, technique-driven, and grounded in parochial scientism. Others remain invested in intricate debates and trajectories in which filmmakers and academics argue about what constitutes a legitimate ethnographic film (e.g., hand-held vs stationary tripod). Instead of adding to this list of concerns and warnings, I seek to engage with video ethnography as a distinctly open-ended epistemological inquiry. In this book, through case studies, I will show how video ethnography offers a great variety of ways through which to explore, record, inflect, and depict lived experiences as part of the kind of searching inquiry and exploration that leads to the production of knowledge.

Video ethnography is capable of producing an immersive, sensuous sense of real life experience that includes aspects of the "sensible sentient" (Merleau-Ponty 1965, p. 179), meaning nuanced experiences of sounds, smells, tastes, and sights that entice, provoke, and summon the senses through what Merleau-Ponty termed "wild being" – the embodied expressions, raw acts of spontaneous immediacy, or banal repetitions that take place in the realm of the experiential world. The dynamics of wild being, according to Merleau-Ponty, are pregnant with a texture, the surface of a depth ... but it does not explain it, does not clarify it, it only concentrates the mystery of its scattered visibility ... [on] the body as sensible and the body as sentient ...

(1965, p. 136)

The sensible sentient as a thing among things implies that sensorial, corporeal bodies are fluid elements connected to an environment, a "flesh among flesh," that interacts in a reciprocal manner – through us, on us, and in us. We cannot extricate ourselves from the fabrics of its flesh. Lived experience, in other words, is reciprocal: we experience and sense ourselves as we are experienced and sensed by the other. This perspective is what Jackson (1998) and Taussig (1993) call "alterity" and "mimesis" as relational experiences rather than detached scientific approaches that attempt to imitate or reproduce the real as an entity awaiting discovery that is "out there." Video ethnography's strength lies in its capacity to simulate and mediate this embodied, immersive shared or relational sensuousness or "mimesis." It also excels at conveying a sense of the relational through the other that we become aware of our sensible and sentient selves. Video ethnographers are able to turn audiovisual attention to these sensorial dimensions of experiential life that reside as "the flesh of the world" (Merleau-Ponty 1965) – by attending to the sounds, sights, textures, and movements around them as they film and in later stages of filmmaking, in postproduction.

Media ethnography

Media anthropologists such as Michael Taussig (1993), Michael Chion (1994), and John Jackson (1998) have all extensively written about the idea of the intersubjective when discussing relationships between lived experience, verisimilitude, contingency, and the somatic domain. Intersubjectivity is an idea that filmmaker anthropologist Sniadecki (2014, p. 35) has also discussed, describing it as "the nexus of shifting social dynamics and affective dimensions *between* human subjects that entails both compassion and conflict" (Sniadecki 2014, pp. 23–27). Jackson (1998, p. 2) calls intersubjectivity "one of the most ubiquitous and persistent questions in human life." He considers lived experience an intersubjective and intercorporeal process, drawing from Merleau-Ponty and John Dewey to discuss its tension and harmony, conflict and conformity (centrifugal and centripetal forces) and asserting: "We must not misconstrue intersubjectivity as a synonym for shared experience, empathic understanding or fellow-feeling. For my purposes, intersubjectivity embraces centripetal and centrifugal forces, and constructive and destructive extremes without prejudice" (Jackson 1998, p. 4).

I am interested in intersubjectivity in relation to video ethnography because filmmakers tend to share the same sensuous environment with their subjects, mediating this intersubjective affect to the screen for audiences to experience. Intersubjectivity does not necessarily mean mutual or shared understanding, but manifests affectively through mutual acknowledgement, and through shared experience of sensuous forms of sound, media, or aspects of communication – wind, gestures, colors, and growls are all sensuous aspects to a soundscape that are experienced primarily by the senses. As Jackson puts it, "It is perhaps truer to say that when one is most deeply involved in what is closest at hand, the entire world is *experienced* ..." (Jackson 1998, p. 15).

Jackson (1998, p. 11) draws from Merleau-Ponty (1965, p. 362) to integrate corporeal and somatic experience into his analysis of intersubjectivity:

> intersubjectivity is not simply a dialectic of conceptual intentions; it is lived as intercorporeity and through the five senses as introceptivity ... We are embodied social beings before we are anything else. The social is already there when we come to know or judge it,

he writes; "it exists obscurely and as a summons." Video ethnography's focus on lived experience – and its corollaries intercorporeity and introceptivity – grounds the "I and other" in the immersive sensuous shared fabric of human, animal, and object extra-subjective encounters.

Jackson also argues that the notion of "negative capability," to coin the English Romantic poet Keats's phrase, "be built into our way of thinking" (Jackson 1998, p. 14) when exploring lived experience through ethnography. Uncertainties also exist even within the sensuously anchored world of wild being. In a footnote referencing Keats, Jackson (1998, p. 14) argues for remaining open to the possibility of the mysterious or inexplicable when creating ethnographies. Castaing-Taylor offers a similar understanding in his discussion of his practice:

> Reality has a magnitude that will always exceed our representations of it and our capacity to understand it. The challenge when you make a work of art is to do the same thing: to come up with an aesthetic object or experience that people will argue over constantly, irreducible to something that can be summarised in a single representation. You watch a documentary and you know what it's saying, what its point of view is. To me that's an abdication of aesthetic, intellectual and political responsibility, because it's reducing the world to something that the filmmaker is pretending to be able to give you certain pronouncements about, to edify the audience.[6]

Video ethnography and wild experience

Dewey, Merleau-Ponty, Keats, Jackson, and Castaing-Taylor all, in different ways, give space to the uncertainties and mysteries of lived experience as part of a general interpretation of the definition or meaning of wild being. Castaing-Taylor incorporates the idea of negative capability by name as central to the core philosophy of the SEL, responding in an interview with Scott MacDonald:

I think it's true that the SEL is also opposed, though this time in the name of art and its inherent exegetical ambiguity – in the name, that is to say, of the figural and its opacity, over against the discursive and its desire for transparency – to the clarity and interpretive self-sufficiency to which anthropology and academia typically tend, and is much more invested in what John Keats, in his famous letter to his brother, characterized as "negative capability" – the quintessentially human capacity to be, as he put it, "in uncertainties, Mysteries, doubts without any irritable reaching after fact & reason."[7]

While I have so far in this introductory chapter primarily cited Merleau-Ponty's notion of wild being in my discussion of video ethnography's central approach to mediating lived experience, I also wish to refer to John Dewey's book *Art as Experience* (1934), because it is here that we can read about his concepts of "having an experience" and "half-knowledge," ideas that belong to the same family of ideas as "wild" and that together are all in some way related to Keats's notion of "negative capability." As Castaing-Taylor explains,

> The idea of making a documentary that provides an interpretation of the world is a very peculiar notion if you think about it. It's very odd if documentaries are claiming to have some privileged purchase on reality, on lived experience. Our desire was simply to give an experience of an experience.[8]

I'm also aware that I have used a term that is inherently ambiguous in this book, when I use the word "wild." If "wild" is usually presented in opposition to the domestic, tame, and rational then it is also something else: it is unpredictable. Wild means appearing, disappearing, and reappearing in the most unusual places at the most unexpected times. In this sense, wild can mean suggestive, changing, and dynamic, open-ended, unlike a piece of voice-over or a more rhetorical or explanatory kind of communication. Castaing-Taylor writes:

> If you watch a film, it's just these shards, these tiny fragments that are put there in a sequence – fragments of sounds and images that the viewer constructs a hypothetical universe out of. It's a kind of domesticated totality, and in this film we're just proceeding with these fragments but not trying to domesticate them into something that's super-linear or something that could be expressed linguistically.[9]

What Castaing-Taylor describes is how video ethnography as a craft tends to preserve the feeling of a lived experience that is prelinguistic, precognitive, prereflective – and never fixed or completely apparent. Video ethnography, to paraphrase Vannini (2014a), attempts to evoke aspects of lived or wild experience.

Video ethnography evokes lived experience and transforms it, through editing, into an assemblage of fragments of sounds and images without overly controlling or reducing the wildness of these experiences and preserving a sense of alterity.

We can therefore describe video ethnography as an inflected transfiguration of an experience into an expressive media gesture of aesthetic knowledge. Lived expressive experience retains elements of its wild properties in a constructed format as a video ethnography; it is through the audiovisual medium that video ethnography invites audiences to interpretively add their own experience and interpretative responses to the documentary through the lens of their own subjective experiences. Audiences form a large part of the dynamic process of video ethnography, because they are on the receiving end of video ethnography's wild characteristics and because this wildness lives on affectively in the bodies of audiences as they watch, listen, and feel. *Video Ethnography* argues for the cultivation of a mediated approach to lived experience that evokes and transforms its wild experience through digital editing. The result is an ethnographic documentary that sometimes enters the public sphere, through which audiences add to its experience.

Wild rules

It is perhaps no coincidence that several of the movies discussed in this book are also situated in wild spaces. *Sweetgrass* is set in wild lands where sheep and humans are actors in a continuous narrative of cross-mountain movement, an interspecies journey of animal–human tensions that at times are full-blown conflicts. *Leviathan* is situated on a fishing vessel inside a wild zone apparently devoid of regulations, where fisherman work 22 arduous hours a day, employed in one of the most dangerous occupations in the world. Here, as wild fish populations are destroyed, wild experiences proliferate as an oceanic wilderness is rapidly emptied by virtual technologies of wildlife surveillance. Both films are examples of video ethnographies that preserve the wild qualities of their subjects through remaining open-ended and "wild." One of this book's main concerns is to consider how ideas, academic training, scholarly knowledge, practice, and methodology might be allowed to go feral or "rewilded," retaining wild (not reckless) properties within domesticated institutional domains such as sociological scholarship. SEL is one pertinent example of how this rewilding is taking place; SEL has even earned the reputation of being wild.[10] What is to be gained by such rewilding?

This book will explore a rich world of wild ethnographic sensibility, *not reckless*, but attentive and attuned to unpredictable situations and unknown outcomes; capable of mediating lived experience with raw immediacy. Such films almost always carry self-reflexive traces and residues of the filmmakers' encounters and the sensibilities that indicate something of the wild conditions under which the projects were created.

Outline of video ethnography

Chapter 1 of this book makes the epistemological claim that video ethnography is a distinct form of aesthetic knowledge that provides a specific way of *knowing, relating and understanding* through sensorial encounters and contact with people, objects, animals, and/or situations. In this chapter I explore the ideas of several theorists, including Merleau-Ponty (1965), Dewey (1934), Sobchack (1992), Marks (2000), and MacDougall (2006), within a continuous overarching thematic frame that focuses on the characteristics of lived experience to discuss how certain aspects and properties are best cinematically evoked and understood.

Chapter 2 transitions into an exploration of contemporary approaches to video ethnography through an analysis of Harvard University's SEL, founded by Lucien Castaing-Taylor. Movies produced by the SEL place viewers *in the experience*, encouraging them to inhabit the film's environment through their bodies. This chapter identifies four characteristics of lived experience ripe for ethnographic filmmaking.

Chapter 3 analyzes the editing techniques of the video ethnographies *Sweetgrass* and *Leviathan*, as case studies that have developed out of the SEL.

Chapter 4 analysis the documentary film *Sanctuary* as a case study in non-human human relationships. The chapter argues that video ethnography offers an aesthetic approach to crafting and evoking knowledge that pushes the boundaries of scholarship into sensuous realms that go beyond words. In the case of *Sanctuary* the theme of healing from neglect and harm is mediated through the figure of the donkey as a beast that has iconic standing as an animal typically subjected to hard labor and to abuse. It calls into question taken-for-granted notions of what "counts" as scholarship, thereby expanding methodological and epistemological boundaries, and in the case of *Sanctuary* it does so beyond the human subject.

Chapter 5 explores examines the documentary film *Girl Model* as a case study of video ethnography. It delves into aspects of lived experience that video ethnography is capable of evoking beyond words, and explains how audiovisual (sensory) knowledge production differs from the written text. This chapter concludes with ethical discussions on suggestions of how images and sound merge as a technique to "rewild" ethnography.

Chapter 6 explores the increasing role of film festivals as a platform for the circulation of video ethnographies that help create the public sphere. When viewers experience immersive video ethnographies in a public sphere there are new possibilities for knowledge production that stretch beyond the academy. This chapter provides a discussion of the ethics of video ethnography by exploring the documentary *Kamp Katrina* as a case study of experiential ethics. It concludes with a call to expand video ethnographies in the social sciences as a form of knowledge production.

Notes

1 http://ohcomely.co.uk/stories/2012/10/18/an-interview-with-directors-lucien-castaing-taylor-and-paravel.
2 www.nytimes.com/2012/09/02/movies/harvard-filmmakers-messy-world.html?pagewanted=all&_r=0.
3 www.ohcomely.co.uk/blog/799.
4 www.ohcomely.co.uk/blog/page/17.
5 Mighty Movie Podcast by Dan Persons.
6 www.ohcomely.co.uk/blog/799.

7 www.frameworkonline.com/festivals/nyff2012/sweetgrass-ilisa-barbash-and-lucien-castaing-taylor.html.
8 www.ohcomely.co.uk/blog/799.
9 www.ohcomely.co.uk/blog/799.
10 See Viennale Film Festival: www.viennale.at/en/series/special-sensory-ethnography-lab; "Within a few years, a department at Harvard University in Boston, USA, has become one of the most interesting and exciting production facilities for current documentary cinema in the world. The so-called Sensory Ethnography Lab (SEL), however, is not a department for classic documentary film in the strict sense of the word, but rather an open place for cinematographic research and experiments. It is a seismographic laboratory of images and sounds that has largely distanced itself from conventional documentary practices and ethnographic ideas, creating its own, fascinating cosmos of audiovisual productions. The Viennale is the first international festival to dedicate a special program to SEL, documenting the wide variety and sensory fascination of this lab's various working methods and productions. In recent years, several films created in Harvard have attracted great international attention and received a number of prizes, including *SWEETGRASS* by Ilisa Barbash and Lucien Castaing-Taylor, *FOREIGN PARTS* by Véréna Paravel and J.P. Sniadecki, *LEVIATHAN* by Véréna Paravel and Lucien Castaing-Taylor, and, most recently, Stephanie Spray's and Pacho Velez's *MANAKAMANA*, which was awarded a Golden Leopard at the 2013 Locarno Film Festival. From the rural work with flocks of sheep to the micro-economics of spare-part car dealership in Brooklyn, from industrial fishing to pilgrimage traditions in Nepal – the realities and worlds that SEL films devote themselves to and explore are as rich, surprising and multi-faceted as the sensory approaches and specific cinematic work of the filmmakers themselves."

1

PHENOMENOLOGY OF CINEMATIC EXPERIENCE

Chapter 1 contextualizes the philosophical precursors that inform a methodology of video ethnography, with its special focus on evoking lived experiences in sensorious ways, reminiscent of Merleau-Ponty's (1965) notion of "perception." Perception, as Merleau-Ponty defines it, is not limited to vision, but occurs through various bodily encounters

> before it has been reduced to a set of manageable, disposable significations;
> ... it addresses itself to that compound of the world and of ourselves that
> precedes reflection, because the examination of the significations in themselves would give us the world reduced to our idealizations and our syntax.
>
> *1965, p. 102*

Merleau-Ponty's writings on experience, or "the flesh of the world," serve as a useful philosophical, methodological guide in all video ethnography work. Sensuousness is a way of relating in the world through the body as a way of knowing and understanding.

Bodies are inseparable from the flesh of the world since corporeality is woven into lived experience. The body inhabits lived experience and, inherently, experience infuses our bodies and allows them to sense aromas, winds, sights, sounds, and flavors. The flesh of the world produces ongoing experiences that bring bodies into contact with others and with environments through sensory encounters. The sound of a dog barking, the braying of a donkey, the shooting of a gun, the sounds of domestic abuse, the falling of rocks, the violence of a thunderstorm – all these experiences bring bodies into the world's sensuous encounter. Sensuousness provides an awareness of our existence in relation to the other, and therefore enlivens our bodies and our consciousness through the magnitude of wonder. Merleau-Ponty (2012, pp. 351–354) states:

> If I experience this inhering of my consciousness in its body and in its world, the perception of other people and the plurality of consciousness no longer present any difficulty … [It] is precisely my body which perceives the body of another, and discovers in that other body a miraculous prolongation of my own intentions, a familiar way of dealing with the world.

The flesh of the world subsumes and envelops consciousness by orientating experiences through the body. Consciousness, movements, and experience all occur through expressive embodied encounters. Mutually intertwined, we sense the flesh of the world sensing us. We are sensible and sentient, and exist at the intersection of these two qualities through what Merleau-Ponty calls the "chiasm of wild being."

Wild being

The sensible and sentient reside in experiential conditions that Merleau-Ponty describes as "Brute Being" (1965, p. 110) and "Wild Being" (1965, pp. 169–170). "[We] must find again in their wild state what answers to our essences and our significations" (Merleau-Ponty 1965, p. 110).

> The effective, present, ultimate and primary being, the thing itself, are in principle apprehended in transparency through their perspectives, offer themselves therefore only to someone who wishes not to have them but to see them, not to hold them as with forceps, or to immobilize them as under the objective of a microscope, but to let them be and to witness their continued being – to someone who therefore limits himself to giving them the hollow, the free space they ask for in return, the resonance they require, who follows their own movement, who is therefore not a nothingness the full being would come to stop up, but a question consonant with the porous being which it questions and from which it obtains not an *answer*, but a confirmation of its astonishment.
> *Merleau-Ponty 1965, pp. 101–102*

   Video ethnography as a methodology seeks to amplify this seam that connects chiasm and directly lived sensuousness. An experiential approach acknowledges the researcher's corporeality as part of the flesh (experience) and therefore does not start from a general theory or external position to survey it. Rather, video ethnographers attempt to refract, record, and evoke experiential phenomena inside a field of sensed-sentience. Video ethnography recouples sentience with the sensory, what Merleau-Ponty called "Brute Being" with nature, and, like more-than-representational theory, assuming that subject and object are sensorially interconnected. In this subject-object blended field of sensorial relations, video ethnographers record lived experiences, erratic movements, and object relations with intuitive reflexivity, attunement, and sensible skills, using audiovisual technology. These lived experiences can be described as "Brute" encounters.

Our discussion of the negative announces to us another paradox of philosophy, which distinguishes it from every problem of cognition and forbids us to speak in a philosophy of a *solution*: as an approach to the far-off as far-off, it is also a question put to what does not speak. It asks of our experience of the world what the world is before it is a thing one speaks of and which is taken for granted, before it has been reduced to a set of manageable, disposable significations; it directs this question to our mute life, it addresses itself to that compound of the world and of ourselves that precedes reflection, because the examination of the significations in themselves would give us the world reduced to our idealizations and our syntax … Hence it is a question whether philosophy as reconquest of brute or wild being can be accomplished by the resources of the eloquent language, or whether it would not be necessary for philosophy to use language in a way that takes from its power of immediate or direct signification in order to equal it with what it wishes all the same to say.

Merleau-Ponty 1965, pp. 102–103

Video ethnography is therefore a methodology that recognizes interwoven sensible sentience in all intermixed "Brute" phenomena – people, places, objects, and animals – gathering up in its path all the ranges and textures of experience and relationships between all these aspects of lived experience. Video ethnography tends to avoid hierarchies of sense and tends not to rely on traditional scholarly forms of discursive explanation or ordering of material.

Aiming at the real: the language of experience

As a methodology, video ethnography does not set out to represent experience, but is instead dedicated to evoking raw experience from an embodied starting point (i.e., in the body of the filmmaker). It's not only audiovisual technology that records and transmits experience through a multisensory and interactive process, but the filmmaker's body and those who he or she meets through encounters. As Merleau-Ponty describes, we are best able to understand and experience "the flesh of the world" by immersing ourselves within its sensuous, expressive, and perceptive properties. We grasp at and are grasped by its ever-shifting refractions by evoking encounters. Video ethnographers soak themselves in "the universe of brute being and … coexistence" (Merleau-Ponty 1965, p. 101).

Merleau-Ponty's critique of essentialism is relevant here: "One practices an 'essentialist' thought which refers to significations beyond experience" (Merleau-Ponty 1965, p. 186). A methodology of video ethnography aims to reassemble experience while being "abound in the sensible world" (Merleau-Ponty 1965, pp. 92–95). "Brute" or "Wild Being" is about embedding practice in lived experiences.

It is to experience therefore that the ultimate ontological power belongs … Significations or essences do not suffice themselves, they overtly refer to our acts of ideation which have lifted them from a brute being, wherein we must find again in their wild state what answers to our essences and our significations.

Merleau-Ponty 1965, pp. 100–110

The type of video ethnography I advocate for as a methodology is attentive to "Wild" or "Brute" experience. For example, when filming video ethnographers inhabit all their senses to relate to the open-ended situation.

Unlike traditional approaches to ethnographies that include interviews, survey research, quantitative analysis, or content analysis, video ethnographies tend to place themselves directly into raw experience, gathering it whole and without framing questions or narrowing its plenitude. Video ethnographers do not place themselves above or outside of experience, or stand apart from experience as an all-seeing eye. Experience is always fluid, unfolding, and transforming, and therefore cannot be generalized.

In other words, video ethnographers adhere to Merleau-Ponty's ideas about experience as irreducible by representational methods. Experience is not easily quantifiable because it is always in flux and continuously changing its sensory variations. It is on the move and it is felt in different ways as it shifts. These porous encounters form the fabric of experience where the sensible meets the sensed. Merleau-Ponty refers to this cohesiveness of touch as chiasm, a "unique space which separates and reunites, which sustains every cohesion" (1965, p. 187).

For Merleau-Ponty, the sounds of our environment – waves, forests, ant rustlings, thunder, the mechanical rumbling of machines, and so on – are facets of acoustic language that register through the body as perception and expression. "Language is everything, since it is the voice of no one, since it is the very voice of the things, the waves, and the forests" (Merleau-Ponty 1965, p. 155). Video ethnography records and transfigures the physical acoustics of lived experience. Video ethnography records the motions, sounds, shapes, and colors as a language of sensuousness that touches the living body. The ethnographic documentary refracts traces of lived experience. As a methodology, video ethnography evokes lived experiences using technology, assembles it aesthetically, and depicts it as sensuous knowledge that is aesthetic, or "felt"– it is relational and shared.

John Dewey: art as experience

Another useful methodological frame stems from Dewey's chapter in his book *Art as Experience* (1934), Chapter 2.2 "The Live Creature and 'Etherial Things'" which focuses on sensory knowledge and on uncertainty, or knowledge that can't be explained through reason or fact – a kind of knowledge that video ethnography fosters. Dewey adopts Keats' interpretation of Shakespeare's "negative capability" to frame his argument. If negative capability is when a writer or thinker is "capable of being in uncertainties, mysteries, doubts, without irritable reaching after fact and reason," then video ethnography, which incorporates intuition, doubt, uncertainty, and mystery in its sensuousness approach to experience, is also related to the idea of imaginative space. The imaginative space that the sensuousness of video ethnography fosters opens up the possibility of what James Agee calls the "cruel radiance of what is." Dewey argues that this vexing feeling of not knowing or being forced to reside in uncertainty can be an intense form of perception, that merges uncertainty, doubt, half-knowledge, and lived experience to turn "experience upon itself to deepen and intensify its own qualities – to imagination and art" (Dewey 1934, p. 35) Dewey refers to this sensuous process as "having an experience."

Having an experience

An experience, according to Dewey, is a continuous unbroken duration that takes place in time and space with a beginning, middle, and end. A methodological tactic often used by video ethnographers to record and understand "an experience" is the long-take or extended sequence. An extended sequence is a continuous unbroken shot, recorded over a prolonged duration of time, which captures part of an experience. Experience consists of sensorial interactions – sounds, motions, activities – that fluctuate as amorphous encounters between subject and object, the seen and unseen, the heard and unheard. These engrossing encounters involve rapid metamorphoses that form part of the excitement and dynamism of aesthetic experience.

Dewey's ideas form a crucial underpinning to the methodological evolution of ideas and practices that inform video ethnography as I present it in this book. Reading and thinking about Dewey's ideas greatly helps to single out and identify some of the capacities of video ethnography that make it so different to traditional forms and media for ethnography. By reimagining experience in aesthetic terms – a living fabric that people, objects, and animals expressively enact – video ethnographers are able to use their own bodies and technology to evoke what Dewey refers to here:

> Experience in this vital sense is defined by those situations and episodes that we spontaneously refer to as being "real experiences"; those things of which we say in recalling them, "that was an experience." It may have been something of tremendous importance – a quarrel with one who was once an intimate, a catastrophe finally averted by a hair's breadth … In such experiences, every successive part flows freely, without seam and without unfilled blanks, into what ensues … There are pauses, places of rest, but they punctuate and define the quality of movement. They sum up what has been undergone and prevent its dissipation and idle evaporation. Continued acceleration is breathless and prevents parts from gaining distinction. In a work of art, different acts, episodes, occurrences melt and fuse into unity, and yet do not disappear and lose their own character as they do so.
>
> *Dewey 1934, p. 36*

Sniadecki (2014, p. 27) has also cited Dewey's approach to lived experience as a facet of video ethnography. He argues that Dewey

> expands aesthetics beyond the confines of the highly specialized, and commodified, realm of fine art and its cultivated appreciation by an educated few, and locates it within the rhythms and activities of the everyday, thereby investing aesthetic experience with new, broader significance and relevance beyond galleries, museums, and universities.

Aesthetic experience is part of the dynamic routine of everyday living and, according to Dewey, "one must begin with it in the raw" (Dewey 1934, p. 4). Examples include "the sights that hold the crowd: the fire-engine rushing by; the machines excavating enormous holes in the earth; the human-fly climbing the steeple-side; the men perched high in the air on girders, throwing and catching red-hot bolts" (Dewey 1934, p. 5). The indexicality of everyday raw and immediate sensorial experience in everyday spaces, for example, a factory, a trawler, a junkyard, or a festival, accumulate as aesthetic experience that sensuously expands the imagination (Sniadecki 2014, p. 27).

As Dewey (1934, p. 267) writes:

> aesthetic experience is imaginative ... It is what happens when varied materials of sense quality, emotion, and meaning come together in a union that marks a new birth in the world ... When old and familiar things are made new in experience, there is imagination. When the new is created, the far and strange become the most natural inevitable things in the world. There is always some measure of adventure in the meeting of mind and universe, and this adventure is, in its measure, imagination.

Video ethnography plunges into aesthetic experience in ways that can make the familiar unfamiliar, the unfamiliar familiar, and the familiar strange – approaches that allow audiences and the filmmaker to see and hear experience anew. When filmed and edited with this kind of immersive intent, video ethnographies demonstrate Dewey's ideas about imagination and aesthetic experience and support Dewey's theory of aesthetics.

It is also worth noting Dewey's idea that sensuousness is ripe with what he calls "vital organization" (Dewey 1934, p. 57). Video ethnography works with lived experience as a material by shaping (editing) it with vital intimacy. When video ethnographers choose to inhabit lived sensuous experience in all its ambiguity and flux they fulfill Dewey's idea that "In such an experience, every successive part flows freely, without seam and without unfilled blanks, into what ensues" (Dewey 1934, p. 37). If experience consists of a continuous merging of interactions, events, and activities, with rest and ruptures that mark the push and pull rhythms of lived experience then video ethnographers explore "an experience" as a series of continuous movements, with dynamic change as "a consummation of a movement" (Dewey 1934, p. 39). There are numerous examples of video ethnographies that illustrate these ideas of merged continuous movement. Sheep and humans move together across mountains (*Sweetgrass*); sea creatures and nets are caught up together inside a deep ocean (*Leviathan*); donkeys interact and comingle day after day together (*Sanctuary*). These examples amply demonstrate that video ethnography is capable of mediating the whole fabric of experience with a highly watchable and absorbing aesthetic vitality that remains true to the experience evoked.

Vitality and properties of images and sounds: Merleau-Ponty and Dewey

Merleau-Ponty and Dewey both posit that there is no distinction between lived and aesthetic experience. Ongoing participatory immersion is necessary in order to evoke the aesthetics of raw experience (Dewey 1934, p. 51). Immersion is inherently part of the process of evoking this kind of raw, immediate aesthetic experience. Researchers who practice video ethnography are doing much more than simply "recording" experience as they document it. Their methodology or approach is bodily, and involves how they move their bodies, how they embrace the camera as an extension of the body, where they place the camera, how and what they hear and choose to listen to while they record, how they learn to feel experience and are touched by experience, and how they choose to embody the dynamics of the situation. Attuning oneself as a video ethnographer to this fabric of experiences is an intimate relationship between body, camera, and subjects who all share the experience differently. Immersion is crucial to how ethnographers cumulatively shape and evoke lived experience as they observe, interact with, become a part of, transform, and evoke its "Wild" aesthetics.

To slightly paraphrase Dewey (1934, p. 112), the material out of which the sound, motion, and image (i.e., the video ethnography) is composed belongs to the common, shared world rather than to the self. Yet there is inevitably self-expression in the video ethnography that can be called "art" because it is made by an individual (and filmmaking team, including editor and sound editor) out of material in a distinctive way in order to present it to the public world as a form of art. Mixing lived experiences, synesthetic matter, and aesthetics all reflect Merleau-Ponty's notion of "Wild Being." Dewey shares with Merleau-Ponty the same approach to the idea of vitality and flux "because the manner in which general material is rendered transforms it into a substance that is fresh and vital. What is true of the producer is true of the perceiver" (Dewey 1934, p. 112). No two perceivers, or audience members, will ever have the same experience, meaning that a new experience is created during each viewing, and simultaneously, a new version of the ethnographic video project is created: "every individual brings ... a way of seeing and feeling that in its interaction with old material creates something new, something previously not existing in experience" (Dewey 1934, p. 113).

The sensuous immediacy of "Wild Being" connects Merleau-Ponty and Dewey's quest to embed the "there is" in the experiential world.

> What is there? What is the *there is*? These questions call not for a conclusion, but for acceptance that ... "It is the experience ... still mute which we are concerned with leading to the pure expression of its own meaning."
>
> *Merleau-Ponty 1965, p. 129 citing Husserl*

"... In a sense the whole of philosophy, as Husserl says, consists in restoring a power to signify, a birth of meaning, or a wild meaning, an expression of experience by experience ..." (Merleau-Ponty 1965, p. 155). Merleau-Ponty's statement resembles Dewey's articulation of "an experience of an experience."

Dewey, echoing Merleau-Ponty, suggests that any art work is both a work of experience and a work of art because of *sensible touch*. All art, whether in the form of video ethnography, painting, music, or stone masonry, is recreated each time it is experienced. In this way, sensible or sensing viewers of video ethnographies or audiences, are part of the experience of the film. Films (and projection or screening equipment) produce experiential affects and also create a material transformation on the body through their presentation of sounds, motion, and sights. Bundling sensations into an artwork, video ethnographies touch viewers through the fabric and waves of the human body's connective tissues. Each viewing reveals a new experience unlike the previous one. Video ethnography can "expand our perception of the natural and material world" (Rust et al., 2013, p. 91).

In this sense, video ethnography or cinema is also in some sense alive and affective. It creates material changes and modulates experiential contact. Its experiential contact acts on the human body. It contains and provokes sensations, affect, and produces new forms of experiences through the viewer's body. In these ways video ethnography differs vastly to ethnographies delivered using the written or spoken word. Here, I turn to Vivian Sobchack to explore her ideas about recording, understanding, and editing video ethnography.

Vivian Sobchack: media ethnography, acts of sensing

If video ethnography restores to audiences a sense of the plentitude of wild experience, conveying the properties of wild experience as lived, perceptive, expressive, immediate, and sensuous, then as Sobchack (1992, pp. 3–4) points out, echoing Merleau-Ponty:

> More than any other medium of human communication the moving picture makes itself sensuously and sensibly manifest as the expression of experience by experience. A film is an act of seeing that makes itself seen, an act of hearing that makes itself heard, an act of physical and reflective movement that makes itself reflexively felt and understood.

Sobchack (1992, p. 5) refers to this process as

> cinema expressing life ... Indeed, it is the mutual capacity for and posses-
> sion of experience through common structures of embodied existence,
> through similar modes of being-in-the-world, that provide the intersub-
> jective basis of object cinematic communication ... The film has the cap-
> acity and competence to signify, to not only have sense but also to make
> sense through a unique and systemic form of communication.

Sobchack (1992, p. 10) suggests that

> watching a film is both a direct and mediated experience of direct experi-
> ence as mediation ... We can see the seeing as well as the seen, hear the
> hearing as well as the heard, and feel the movement as well as see the
> moved ... The cinema thus transposes what would otherwise be the invis-
> ible, individual, and intersubjective privacy of direct experience as it is
> embodied into the visible, public, and intersubjective sociality of a lan-
> guage of direct embodied experience ... A film simultaneously has sense
> and makes sense both for us and before us ... It gives birth to and actual-
> izes signification, constituting and making manifest the primordial signifi-
> cance that Merleau-Ponty called "wild meaning" – the pervasive and as
> yet undifferentiated significance of existence as it is lived rather than
> reflected upon.

Along with the far-reaching sensuous possibilities of experiencing cinema as lived
experience, audiences will also have various interpretations and experiences,
adding to the expansive range of video ethnography's experiential intelligence.

Relating ideas from phenomenology to the practice of video ethnography,
according to Sobchack (1992, p. 28), has many benefits because, "as a research
procedure, phenomenology calls us to a series of systematic reflections within
which we question and clarify that which we intimately live, but which has
been lost to our reflective knowledge through habituation and/or institutionalization." Sobchack suggests that lived experiences become reified by quantitative
analysis and after-the-fact explanations and that phenomenology attempts to
reanimate what has been

> institutionally sedimented. And, because it turns us toward the origins of
> our experience of phenomena and acknowledges both the objective and
> enworldedness of phenomena and the subjective embodiment experiencing
> of them, such radical reflection opens up not only fresh possibilities for
> reflective knowledge, but also fresh possibilities of living knowledge and
> experiencing phenomena, for seeing the world and ourselves in a critically
> aware way.
>
> *Sobchack 1992, p. 28*

Video ethnographies allow audiences to directly sense and interpret encounters beyond written text. In this way, video ethnography as ethnographic cinema creates a "shared space of being, of seeing, hearing, and bodily and reflective movement performed and experienced by both film and viewer" (Sobchack 1992, p. 10). The haptic contact produced in this viewing experience is further explored by Laura Marks (2000) in her contribution to reflections about phenomenology and video ethnography.

Laura Marks: haptic ethnography

Marks adopts Merleau-Ponty's ideas about embodied spectatorship, by way of Sobchack, to explore phenomenological viewing experiences. In this section, I explore how Marks' theories contribute to video ethnography's methodological approach by directing attention to the convergence between sensible touch and what Marks calls *haptic visuality*. Haptic visuality, according to Marks (2000, p. xi), is the "... way vision itself can be tactile, as though one were touching a film with one's eyes." In haptic visuality, the camera is placed up close to glide over textured surfaces rather than gazing at them – it elicits feelings about the experience of touch. Marks' haptic approach to the materiality of cinema encourages sensuous engagement between the object (the film) and the viewer who encounters the movie. "Film signifies through materiality, through a contact between perceiver and object represented" (Marks 2000, preface). The object and the viewer work in tandem and on each other through haptic contact. Drawing from Sobchack, Marks suggests that "cinema is not an illusion but an extension of the viewer's embodied existence ... It stresses the interactive character of film viewing" (Marks 2000, p. 149). In other words, film isn't only intellectual, verbal, or thesis driven, it is experienced through the whole body – the body perceives cinema ... "Our perceptions fold us back into this thick world at the same time as they demarcate us from it ... It is not I who touch, it is my body" (Marks 2000, p. 147).

Marks (2000, p. 2) suggests that haptic cinema evokes "memories both individual and cultural, through an appeal to nonvisual knowledge, embodied knowledge, and experiences of the senses, such as touch, smell, and taste." Haptic images "invite the viewer to respond to the image in an intimate, embodied way, and thus facilitate the experience of other sensory impressions as well" (Marks 2000, p. 2). Marks' ideas help inform the practice of video ethnography as a methodology concerned with evoking the experience of texture and *touch*, as the camera moves across the surface of materials hapticly as a conductor, producing "affect" through the recording of sensuous, tactile encounters. Affect refers to the change of intensity that occurs on the surface or skin of the body.

Central to video ethnography is Marks' designation of cinema as a *conductive* or a *conductor*. She emphasis the

> tactile and contagious quality of cinema as something we viewers brush up
> against like another body ... The very circulation of a film among different

viewers is like a series of skin contacts that leave mutual traces … To think of film as a skin acknowledges the effect of a work's circulation among different audiences, all of which mark it with their presence.

Marks 2000, preface; p. xii

"Brushing up against" each other creates contact that heightens awareness and involvement. Audiovisual devices can hapticly record the material world as a multisensory, aesthetic experience (Marks 2000, p. 2). "Although cinema is an audiovisual medium, synethesia, as well as haptic visuality, enables the viewer to experience cinema as multisensory … These emerging configurations of sense experience contribute a countercurrent to global culture's increasing simulation of sensory experience" (Marks 2000, p. 23).

All senses work together in the making and viewing of cinema, and video ethnography is well positioned to generate self-reflexive awareness of the role of the senses in sensemaking or knowledge production. Marks refers to "breaking away" from accepted established methods of research. "In order to find expression, emerging thoughts and things must speak in the terms of the discourses that are established, though at the same time they break away from them" (Marks 2000, p. 28). I argue that it is possible to interpret Marks' notion of "breaking away" as what I would call a *wild moment*. By this I mean that breaking away from traditional methods of ethnography helps open up new spaces for ethnographic practice. It is a "sort of dance between sedimented, historical discourses and lines of flight, between containment and breaking free … knowing that the result will be contradictory and partial" (Marks 2000, p. 28).

Marks argues that opening up new spaces – adopting "wild" approaches that go beyond the established territory of ethnography – offers an alternative methodology "within dominant discourses, both cinematic and more broadly cultural, while simultaneously developing the powerful emergent lines of flight that will open them to the outside" (Marks 2000, pp. 28–29). Foucault (1988) refers to this space of opening up "interstice." Interstitial spaces work at the limits to create methodological practices deemed "wild," alien, or unknown. Video ethnography tends to reflect Marks' ideas about haptic cinema and to foster unorthodox or "wild" methodological approaches to open up new ethnographic possibilities. Video ethnography is both perceptive and expressive and it produces outcomes that reveal more than other methods are able to reveal (Marks 2000, p. 29).

Last, Marks (2000, pp. 30–31) argues that any given methodology must be broken up to reveal its blind spots. "I believe it is also possible to talk of an order of the sensible, which, like the seeable and the sayable, is the sum of what is accessible to sense perception at a given historical and cultural moment." Because video ethnography involves haptic experience it often feels more openended than other forms of ethnography and thus tends to feel historically and culturally in flux and readily available.

David MacDougall: contemporary examples

Like his predecessors, MacDougall argues for an experiential approach to movie-making (2006, p. 272). In *The Corporeal Image* he argues that experience is never isolated; it connects and undergoes shifts; and is constantly "becoming" (2006, p. 274). MacDougall suggests that the goal isn't better description but rather "gaining a fuller understanding of the relation of individuals to their societies would seem to require further analysis of the societies themselves as complex sensory and aesthetic environments" (MacDougall 2006, p. 95).

According to MacDougall (1998, p. 272), sensuous media contributes to a new field of *experiential studies* – studies of social knowledge – *experienced* in images and sounds. MacDougall's call for an experiential approach to analyzing societies as complex sensory and aesthetic environments seems to be answered by video ethnography's capacities for evoking the whole fabric of lived experience in all its complexity.

MacDougall suggests that video ethnography's remarkable ability – as a method of ethnographic inquiry – lies in the attention it gives to detail and to the particular, crossing transcultural boundaries by focusing on material and aesthetic experience. Video ethnographic methods create "sudden affinities between ourselves and others apparently different from us" (MacDougall 2006, p. 245). This quote captures video ethnography's ability to invoke a sense of the familiar and the unfamiliar. For example, video ethnography can't show the rules of a culture, but it can show infractions and their consequences, thereby bringing attention to unspoken and unseen gestural rules. MacDougall (2006, p. 264) contends that ethnographic films are inherently transgressive because of their open-endedness. They evoke life experiences and foster active embodied engagement. The subject and object of ethnographic films are "inseparably fused" (MacDougall 2006, p. 265). Video ethnography fosters physical engagement and situates viewers in relation to objects and experiences inside situations (MacDougall 2006, p. 266). Its images and sounds are complex; video ethnographies usually contain words, appearances, and actions inside settings or environments that also have complex acoustic, visual, and kinesthetic dimensions (MacDougall 2000, p. 268). The methodological production of video is a fluid process with vast potential for rupture and suture.

Video ethnography tends to de-emphasize "the cognitive world" (MacDougall 2006, p. 259), instead emphasizing process – the how, not the why. It encourages interpretation that "concerns making, appearing, doing" (MacDougall 2006, p. 259). Video ethnography expresses the immediacy of encounters by producing synesthetic experiences (MacDougall 2006, p. 262). Video ethnography is "often concerned with words as with images, for words are inseparable from the social transactions of everyday life" (MacDougall 2006, p. 269). Pursuing this kind of ethnography allows researchers "to see how words fit into these events, along with postures, gestures, tones of voice, facial expressions, and silences that accompany them" (MacDougall 2006, p. 269). Video ethnography tends to shift emphasis to experiential or "sensory" knowledge – that is, how people perceive their material environment and interact with it, in both its natural and cultural forms, including their interactions with others as physical beings (MacDougall 2006, p. 269). MacDougall refers to this type of sensory knowledge as a "material consciousness" that contains a physical presence as material trace.

The physical presence as material trace is prelinguistic and therefore allows a re-centering of

> corporeal spaces of our own and others' lives – the manner in which we all, as social creatures, assimilate forms and textures through our senses, learn things before we understand them, share experiences with others, and move through the varied social environments that surround us.
>
> *MacDougall 2006, p. 270*

Video ethnography is well suited to amplifying and magnifying interrelations between phenomena – objects, animals, people, places, and times in the world – through encounters.

MacDougall offers four conceptual frameworks for experiential ethnography: topographic, temporal, corporeal, and personal. The topographic framework captures a sense of place and space (the three-dimensional world); sounds are often environmental (and recorded on-site). Sound and image mutually support one another. A temporal framework consists of duration, time, and rituals. The continuity of a temporal shot is recorded as a singular, unbroken flow of continuous movement. A temporal approach relies on patience, participation, and experiential immersion to understand the rhythmic interactions over the course of time. The extended shot "takes in" multiple sources of sound and movement simultaneously, to engage viewers. A corporeal framework focuses on embodiment and on material objects. Postures, gestures, tone, voice, and silence are examples of corporeal encounters.

Long-term projects that explore complex social phenomena in a particular setting from a variety of perspectives are key to MacDougall's ideas (MacDougall 2006, p. 273). He argues that video ethnography as a methodology is ideally suited to exploring people's intimate lives, eked out in rooms, on the street, and in compounds; during journeys taken; capturing dilemmas; objects made and used; sounds heard, faces, fears, pleasures (MacDougall 2006, p. 273). These are intimations of a distinct type of knowledge that develops from a close personal acquaintance with a particular society (MacDougall 2006, p. 273).

Contemporary relevance: a case for video ethnography

Video ethnography records and evokes lived experience through a mediated and embodied understanding of that experience. It demonstrates how lived experience shapes the filmmaker during the making of a project and how shaping is also part of experiential knowledge production. Sniadecki (2014, p. 27) explains,

An image, understood here in the context of media anthropology as at once both pictorial and aural, renders the contiguous physical and affective space of person and place as a *composite*: an evocative assemblage of objects, happenings, and emotions, the sheer indexicality of which takes hold of us, as it were, all at once.

Video ethnography evokes lived experience by accessing its sensuous, corporeal, and embodied properties. Its methodological approach prioritizes existence in the physical, sensuous world of lived experience – the experience of humans, animals, and objects in environments. As a methodological approach to understanding and encountering lived experiences, video ethnography foregrounds sensory experience as a form of knowledge. Sniadecki quotes David MacDougall:

> Just as the anthropologist must insert him- or herself experientially into the process of fieldwork, so the audience must be inserted into the production of the work. This is a perception with close affinity to the cinema. New concepts of anthropological knowledge are being broached in which meaning is not merely the outcome of reflection upon experience but necessarily *includes* the experience. In part, then, the experience *is* the knowledge.
>
> *Sniadecki 2014, p. 27 citing MacDougall 1998, p. 79*

Lived experience involves the immediacy of sensuousness and takes place collectively in mutual, co-determined ways. It unfolds amidst a jumble of merged aesthetic sensations and everyday experiential embodiment. Embodied engagement occurs intersubjectively through encounters and contacts. Video ethnography carefully attends to such encounters, apprehending tactile traces of intersubjective communication – points of sensory contact and convergences of understanding that have a shape, a pattern, and a form, one that is often dramatic. An experiential, arts-based practice inverts the usual approach of studying art and film as an empirical social science endeavor and instead creates and evokes the empirical as artistic social science practice embedded in the field of sensuous and experiential studies. Video ethnography appeals to the senses to engage lived experiences and object-orientated life, thereby exceeding academic institutions' continual reliance on text to engage public audiences.

What is needed, then, is more "Wild," more porous, and fluid ways to explore the flux of lived experiences within video ethnography. As Wood and Brown (2009, p. 521) suggest, it is necessary

> to find a mode of expression capable of capturing and communicating the feelings and perceptual affect of running free in the field ... The branch of philosophy dealing with the study of sensory or emotional values is aesthetics ... Broadly, aesthetics research involves alternative methods of knowledge building

that link practices of the social sciences, humanities and the arts, by attending to the particularities and subjectivity of lived experience.

Video ethnography opens up access and shares sounds, sights, and movements with viewers in linguistic and nonlinguistic ways, thereby extending the range of experiential encounters beyond the linguistic and further expanding the interpretive possibilities of sensory connection. Video ethnography "attempts to renew our approach toward social science research by 'rendering' the aesthetic principles that structure the cultural or symbolic aspects of everyday life as an 'enacted way of knowing and being'" (Springgay et al., 2005, p. 904). In this way, video ethnography allows researchers to explore experience from the *inside* and to make them resonate in haptic and sensible ways that physically touch audiences as they view video ethnographies.

Video ethnography: audiovisual experience as sensemaking

This final section demonstrates how the emergent practice of video ethnography relates to lived experience. As a methodology, video ethnography is the practice of using audiovisual methods to interpretively craft and evoke lived experience as media, or, in other words, it entails making media. As such it differs from the standard ethnographic approach in which scholars study and interpret media made by others. In video ethnography meaning is not "the outcome of reflection on experience but necessarily includes the experience. In part, then, the experience is the knowledge" (MacDougall cited in Sniadecki 2014, pp. 27, 79). Video ethnography's naturalistic grounding in

> interpretive and phenomenological undertakings put[s] a strong premium on the meaningfulness of sensory experiences, the significance of the skillful practices through which we make sense of the world, and the importance of aesthetically-rich expressions through which life-worlds are made and represented.
>
> *Vannini 2014a*

Video ethnography embraces an interpretive analysis of lived experience, and expands written scholarship by actively producing and disseminating audiovisual experiences as sensorial knowledge. The substance of sensory knowledge is the fleeting patterns of lived, aesthetic experiences recorded as movements, sounds, colors, and ambience. Video ethnography explores, records, and crafts these aesthetic experiences into documentary films with interpretive sensibilities that can be disseminated as public knowledge. Video ethnography therefore creates a vibrant, sensible object or artwork (e.g., the documentary film) that can be digitally disseminated as publically available knowledge in various audiovisual formats, in homes, classrooms, and in public venues. Examples of public and privatized venues include the internet (e.g., iTunes, Netflix, Amazon, Hulu, Fandor, Vimeo, online journals), film festivals, DVDs, classrooms, and television. Viewers add to films' aesthetic meanings through all that they bring to the viewing experience.

MacDougall (2006, p. 245) refers to this active aesthetic approach as the "cinematic imagination" in that it involves "a desire to create an interpretive space for the reader or spectator ... Structuring a work in this way involves a multi-positional perspective that acknowledges the fragmentary nature of experience and, by extension, the constructed nature of human knowledge." Open-ended interpretive spaces activate the audience's imagination, allowing viewers to fill in the gaps with "non-language-material" (MacDougall 2006, p. 259). Active interpretation of lived experience in a documentary format can enliven multiple sensory possibilities such as smell, touch, taste, and memory. The methodological crafting of audiovisual experiences as a documentary is what Paul Stoller (1997) calls "sensuous scholarship."

Sensuous scholarship includes an understanding of "how people perceive their material environment and interact with it, in both its natural and cultural forms, including their interactions with others as physical beings" (MacDougall 2006, p. 269). I argue in this book that video ethnography is a legitimate and far-reaching form of sensuous scholarship.

Conclusion: practice of video ethnography

To conclude I will now seek to relate video ethnography's methodological approach to the ideas of the various theorists to which I have referred above. I will now focus on three available methodologies used by video ethnography in the crafting of documentary films, all of which help to contribute aesthetic knowledge: (1) extended sequences; (2) inhabitation; and (3) tacit sensibilities.

Extended sequences

A methodological technique often used by documentary filmmakers to record and understand the continuity of aesthetic experience is the long-take or extended sequence. An extended sequence is a continuous unbroken shot, recorded over a prolonged duration, which evokes varied aesthetic experience (comprising of whatever the camera records during this duration). As Scott Mac-Donald (2014, p. 8) writes, of the Sensory Ethnography Lab's various approaches to documentary filmmaking, which includes use of the long-take: "That which distinguishes an experience as aesthetic is conversion of resistance and tensions, of excitations that in themselves are temptations to diversion, into movement toward an inclusive and fulfilling close."

According to MacDonald, aesthetic documentaries that focus on everyday experience

> reveal how things happened to certain people at a particular time. This experience occurs on two levels simultaneously: we understand that the

subjects in the film are going through specific experiences that we are in some measure witness to, and we, as members of an audience, are experiencing these cinematic versions of the subjects' experiences. Whatever conclusions the subjects might draw from what has happened to them, we, as spectators, must decide not only what their experiences, as rendered through cinema, might have meant to them and to the filmmakers, but what they do mean to us.

MacDonald 2014, p. 9

In the long-take or extended sequence audiences are imaginatively opened up to nuances, rather than encouraged to foreclose them. Their own experience of the extended sequence becomes part of the experience of the documentary film or video ethnography, so that they enter more fully into the experience or world of the video ethnography.

Inhabiting aesthetic experience

As previously discussed in this book, video ethnography immersively inhabits lived experience and video ethnographies tend to incorporate complex cultural and social contexts that are aesthetic (Garrett and Hawkins 2014). Examples of this aesthetic lived experience complexity include perception as an engaged connection; embodied movement as a way to touch and create the material world; and sound as a crucial fabric of experience (MacDougall 2011). These aesthetic experiences can be placed, visually and sonically, in the wider, contentious contexts in which they symbolically and materially occur. In all cases, the important point here is that the ethnographer is not above or outside fields of experience, separate from it as an all-seeing eye, or observing from an omnipotent or objective viewpoint. Rather, ethnographic filmmakers who methodologically immerse themselves in the aesthetic experiences of their subject matter inhabit a common relationship with those in a similar situation.

Tacit sensibility

How the filmmaker holds the camera, where he/she places the camera, how he/she hears or listens to sounds while recording, how he/she encounters experience and embodies the dynamics of a situation, all of these considerations contribute to the methodological crafting of a video ethnography and are facets of what can be called tacit sensibility. Tacit sensibility is the process of developing the ability to use one's body and audiovisual technology in the process of conducting video ethnographies that observe, interact with, hear, and record lived experience by moving through and inhabiting shared space. Consequentially, the documentary, as a vibrant, living object, is an edited accumulation of tacit sensibilities that involve style, sound, movements, gestures, and fluid consideration of aesthetics. Dewey describes this process thus: "Every individual brings with him … a way of seeing and feeling that in its interaction with old material creates something new, something previously not existing in experience" (Dewey 1934, p. 113). Tacit sensibility is an essential component of crafting "Wild" or "Brute" into open-ended aesthetic knowledge. Dewey suggests that a documentary film, as a work of crafted experience, works through sensorial, sensible, or tacit encounters rather than by means of overt, verbal exposition or discursive, rhetorically-based explanation.

This chapter has provided a methodological outline for video ethnography that borrows from Merleau-Ponty, Dewey, Sobchack, and Marks' ideas about the phenomenology of lived aesthetic experience. Video ethnography as a discipline is still in its infancy, having evolved out of the intersection of new media, cinema, and ethnographic sensibilities. Thanks to its open-ended experimental tendencies and self-reflexive exploration of how its ethnographies are shaped, it is already a field that values placing researchers as close as possible to the midst of experiential flux (Harris 2016). Its uses audiovisual devices to produce forms of legitimate aesthetic knowledge that belong alongside textual forms of analysis and ethnographic representation.

Methodologically, video ethnography adapts to dynamic circumstances-in-progress with an open, reflexive, and flexible sensibility rather than through a set of prescriptive and mechanistic rules. Its malleable, non-prescriptive, and porous methodology is based in its propensity to merge and to blend all lived experience and living encounters. Survey and quantitative research are unable to capture these crucial aspects of flux. Video ethnographies are edited, shaped in qualitatively distinct ways, and rendered empirically (Merriman 2014; Mitchell 2011). This approach verges on empirical art, or an "aesthetics of the empirical," in the sense that video ethnography radically aestheticizes empirical observations as new forms of knowledge. Video ethnography facilitates expressive modes of inquiry. In turn, the dynamism of the documentary medium produces sensory knowledge that invites audiences' active engagement as interpreters who bring their own senses and experience to each documentary film.

By crafting the sensuousness and flux of lived experience into a sharable form of media, video ethnography creates a form of "vibrant knowledge." Created out of the very fabric of aesthetic experience, ethnographic documentaries surpass traditional methods, such as interviews, survey research, quantitative analysis, or content analysis, while also reaching a wide public through new avenues of digital distribution. As an emergent form of experiential ethnography that is still struggling to find legitimacy, I argue in this book that video ethnography is currently making an important yet underrecognized contribution to valuable ethnographic research.

2

THE WILD LAB

Sensory ethnography

There is nothing extraordinary about the materials you'll find at Harvard University's Sensory Ethnography Lab (SEL): books, DVDs, a projector, hard drives, wine, beer, and animal skins. Yet, the films that emerge from the SEL are easily some of the most discussed, programmed, and raved-about documentary films each year. The aesthetic approach of the SEL's documentaries falls somewhere between auteur/arthouse cinema, and radically empirical quasi-academic ethnography. Some of the SEL's documentaries approach their subject matter in a seemingly straightforward manner (e.g., *Foreign Parts, Sweetgrass*), while others transmogrify lived experience into a fluctuating, cosmic abstraction couched within a mysterious universe of darkness (e.g., *Leviathan*).

In this chapter I provide a broad overview of some of the SEL's movies' general themes, while demonstrating the filmmakers' immersive approach to an ethnographic cinema grounded in the phenomenology of lived experience, drawing on ideas I discussed in the previous chapter. I also identify several of the SEL's conceptual and concrete aesthetic practices.

I will discuss how the SEL tends to embed its aesthetic practices in lived experience before exploring the SEL's approach to expressive phenomenology and cinematic sensory experience. I begin with John Dewey's concept of "having an experience," a concept I discussed in the previous chapter and that I believe to be central to understanding the experiential approach to filmmaking established by the SEL.

Sensory ethnography lab

Films from the SEL, such as *Sweetgrass, Manakamana, People's Park, Demolition, Foreign Parts, Leviathan, Into the Hinterlands*, and *Single Stream*, have all premiered at top-tier film festivals, received international awards, and have also enjoyed international retrospectives at places such as the Whitney Biennial, Montreal International Documentary Festival (RIDM), and Viennale Film Festival. Internationally recognizable film companies specializing in a unique blend between artistic cinema and academic ethnography have opted to become distributors of these prestigious films. Merging art with empirical ethnography, SEL films embrace experiential aesthetics more vigorously, and rigorously, than perhaps any other example of ethnographic documentaries emerging from the United States since David MacDougall's body of film work spanning three decades, and Robert Gardner's feature documentary *Forest of Bliss* (1986).

The SEL was initiated by its Director, Lucien Castaing-Taylor, who started teaching anthropology at Harvard in 2002. Castaing-Taylor's written publications include *Visualizing Theory* (1994), *Cross-Cultural Filmmaking* (with Barbash 1997), *Transcultural Cinema* (an edited collection of essays by ethnographic filmmaker David MacDougall, 1998), and *The Cinema of Robert Gardner* (coedited with Barbash 2007). He was also the founding editor of the American Anthropological Association's journal *Visual Anthropology Review* (1991–1994). Castaing-Taylor founded the SEL in 2006 to provide students with an opportunity to explore "innovative combinations of aesthetics and ethnography." According to Castaing-Taylor, the goal of the Lab is to

> [use] analog and digital media to explore the aesthetics and ontology of the natural and unnatural world ... SEL provides an academic and institutional context for the development of creative work and research that is itself constitutively visual or acoustic – conducted through audiovisual media rather than purely verbal sign systems – and which may thus complement the human sciences' and humanities' almost exclusive reliance on the written word and quantification.[1]

The establishment of the SEL, I argue, marks the emergence of an "experiential turn" in media ethnography in the United States. The SEL's commitment to integrating brute lived experience and aesthetics is an unabashedly novel approach, especially given how SEL projects rework disciplinary demarcations. In turn, the SEL's reworking of academic boundaries generates new spaces of possibilities for other ethnographically inclined or experientially orientated filmmakers. These spaces include film festivals, television stations, installations in galleries and museums, DVD stores, online digital access points, and, of course, academic institutions, through screenings, libraries, and courses.

In this chapter, I discuss four common methodological approaches found in SEL documentary films that stem from radical phenomenology outlined in the previous chapter. These approaches are (1) experiential immersion, (2) incorporation of the reflexive presence of the ethnographer, (3) inclusion of diegetic sound, and (4) emphasis on relationships or encounters. These characteristics speak to a broader aesthetic movement in academia that arises out of postlinguistic, post-structuralist, and post-cultural theories, something of a return to radical phenomenology as aesthetic practice, coupled with post-representational media labeled as new materialism or more-than-representational theory. As Pels et al. (2002, p. 1) put it,

> After poststructuralism and constructivism have melted everything that was solid into air, it was perhaps time that we noticed once again the sensuous immediacy of the objects we live, work and converse with, in which we routinely place our trust, which we love and hate, which bind us as much as we bind them.

Examples of these objects populate SEL movies: junkyards, trawlers, gondolas, recycled debris, animals, dust, water, and, of course, the films themselves as aesthetic objects. What is distinctive about the SEL's body of work is that all its documentary films involve expressive phenomenology grounded in lived experience, a particular set of values and practices occurring within the realm of video ethnography.

Aesthetics of an experience

The SEL engages with and reconfigures the phenomenology of lived experience under the rubrics of "new materialism." New materialism focuses on the experiential vibrancy of objects, interspecies communication, sensuous knowledge, and the ability to mobilize publics. Coole and Frost (2010) argue that new materialism relocates and places humans within an ecology that is constantly in experiential flux. Intersecting new materialism with sensuous experience can facilitate a more nuanced understanding of how objects become meshed with the environment, humans, and animals. Material culture is the

> whole habitat which encircles us, the physical world entangled with the cultural ... It is an ecology of connections that we negotiate to make our meanings and our livings. In this habitat, cinema is a form of negotiation, a mediation that is itself ecologically placed as it consumes the entangled world around it, and in turn, [is] itself consumed.
>
> *Rust et al., 2013, p. 1*

The phenomenological writings of Merleau-Ponty and experiential writings of Dewey presented in previous chapters help to illuminate the foundations of this approach to film aesthetics.

The SEL often depicts aspects of experiential materiality that entail more-than-human subjects, encompassing interspecies interrelations, aspects of the environment, and vibrant objects. Human bodies are recast as simply one of a number of actors in a wide array of ecologies in which actors of all kind overlap as part of a larger system. SEL films pay more attention to the qualities of lived experience than to expository or explanatory discourse or language, and offer an open-ended interpretation of experiential properties. According to Vannini (2016), these properties include fluid sensuous movements, vitality, hybridity, corporeality, materiality, and ineffability.

> The lifeworld escapes a human grasp keen on authentic reproduction. Therefore rather than represent it, we *evoke* multiple impressions of it. The lifeworld is often mysterious and incomprehensible. As if populated by uncanny presences, the "ghosts" of that lifeworld haunt the non-representational ethnographer, seducing him/her to attempt a thick description and imaginative interpretation that merely flirt back with reality.
>
> *Vannini 2016, p. 14*

The SEL's immersive approach to generating aesthetic ways of knowing and understanding tends to emphasize affective relations, sensuous attention, and fluid relations between corporeality, sentient bodies, the environment, and vitality of brute experience.

At the center of the SEL's sensibility is a focus on aesthetic experience:

> [h]arnessing perspectives drawn from the human sciences, the arts, and the humanities, the aim of SEL is to support innovative combinations of aesthetics and ethnography, with original nonfiction media practices that explore the bodily praxis and affective fabric of human existence. As such, it encourages attention to the many dimensions of social experience and subjectivity that may only with difficulty be rendered with words alone.[2]

Crucial here is the attention directed to nonlinguistic rendering of lived experience and a focus on aural and visual ethnographic media to evoke encounters as aesthetic knowledge. According to Ernst Karel, a social anthropologist and sound artist who manages and teaches at the SEL,

> Most of the work in the SEL is in video, and broadly involves trying to use image and sound to convey something about lived experience in ways specific to the possibilities of sensory media, and which would be difficult if not impossible to do through language alone … So in terms of the influence on my practice, I would say that it reminds me to think of sound work in a larger context of aesthetic and investigative media practices, that sound work need not be only about sound.[3]

In a sense, the SEL approach to video ethnography represents a return to an empirical ethnographic sensibility with an experiential approach. It includes an aesthetic concern with the properties of material objects and life; physicality and temporality – objects of aesthetic interest that have been less in vogue with filmmakers in recent decades, but these were once central preoccupations for filmmakers, ethnographers, and artists. As Véréna Paravel explains,

> Many of the concerns of works coming out of the SEL go back to the beginnings of cinema, Lumière and Melies, to Flaherty and Grierson, to Mead and Bateson and Deren. They are not all new. I think that SEL films for the most part are in some ways in counterpoint to mainstream docs [documentaries]. They're less discursive, less interpretive, more invested in aesthetic opaqueness and the interpretive agency of the viewer. But many filmmakers, whether part of the self-applied avant-garde or experimental traditions or not, also militate against the mainstream.[4]

Paravel's interview offers insight into the aesthetic sensibilities of the SEL's approach to evoking lived experience described in the previous chapter. Notably, their films often eschew interviews, exclude expository information, omit narrative arcs, and refuse to reduce the complexity of lived experience to reflective verbal sound bites. They are not story, plot, or event focused, or discursive in any way. Instead, the SEL's films are committed to a phenomenology of aesthetic experience as directly lived and encountered, and to evoking an environment in which human, object, and interspecies experiences are interlaid as part of an overall ecology or habitat, a material and physical sense of which is strongly conveyed through the film. Projects coming out of the SEL avoid reflecting or representing recorded experience back onto an audience through mirrored imitation of the original. Instead, they enact and interject lived experiences as evocations. These films often transgress and transmogrify the limits of experience, practicing radical mimesis through their transfiguration of the real by way of the aesthetic imagination. Lived experience is presented as an aesthetic, affective gesture or an encounter, rather than as a mirror of the real.

I contend that the SEL's film work foregrounds aesthetics much more centrally than do any other contemporary nonfiction films in the United States. Their encounter-driven immersive approach to lived experience is phenomenologically orientated. All SEL's filmmakers seem committed to imbuing the stream of material properties arising from the locations in which they film with experiential vitality, as though to honor the intensity of sound, texture and the granular details, ambience, and tempo of each place documented. How SEL footage is recorded, how SEL filmmakers approach situations, what style of contact they adopt, where their camera is placed – whether it is still, in motion, or fixed – and how their films are edited to evoke gestural sensuousness, these are all critical elements that contribute to the SEL aesthetic that has become so internationally renowned.

In SEL films the camera seems to become an extension of the SEL filmmaker's body so that audiences feel almost situated within the experience filmed. The SEL filmmaker tends to evoke lived experience in an open-ended way that widens interpretive possibilities rather than foreclosing interpretation.

The SEL filmmaker is buried in their subject matter, rather than commenting as an "objective" researcher analyzing their subject matter. This embedded methodological approach is, in practical filmmaking terms, highly skilled, attuned, and self-reflexive. First, it requires an acute ability to move with subject matter which in turn involves acute attunement to surroundings and an awareness of the experiential rhythms, shapes, and textures of the filmed environment. Filming by seemingly blending into the environment, and letting its experiences unfold, is an ethical position that sets SEL aesthetics apart from more journalistic styles of filmmaking. SEL filmmakers shirk the expository style of establishing shots that attempt to "set up" a situation and instead use the disorienting effect of images and sounds to defamiliarize the familiar, rather than inform, promoting an immersive, sensorially saturating experience for audiences when they experience the film on screen. Strikingly aesthetic, SEL films weave audiences into the very texture of their films' evoked experiences through an aesthetic that prioritizes sensuous immediacy. Diegetic sound contributes to the intense sonic rapport viewers feel with the experience depicted through soundscapes that activate our senses.

This intensely phenomenological approach to evoking the aesthetics of lived experience also leaves "story" or "plot" elements out of the framework. The open-ended ambiguity of SEL films avoids boxing viewers into a closed system of interpretation centered around a narrative arc, and does nothing to distil experience into "signposting" sound bites, or any of the other common devices of character-driven stories. Instead, SEL films allow for a wide range of synesthetic interpretations in ways that allow audiences to participate in the movie's ongoing creation or vitality, each time it is screened. The SEL film tends to feel deliberately strange and unfamiliar, in part because it resists conventional exposition or explanatory modes, instead prioritizing experience itself as an unfolding duration or experience in ways that reconfigure audiences' imaginative relationship with places, people, animals, and ecologies.

SEL cinema's aesthetic creates distancing effects, estrangement, and dissonance, using defamiliarization in ways that permit new perceptions and openness to encounters with lived experience. By refusing to explain, guide, or lecture, SEL films leave audiences to their own thoughts, eschewing the usual props of voiceover, title cards, or other forms of signposting. As audiences watch they may try to orientate themselves with questions like, "Where am I?" "What is happening?" These questions activate viewers as participatory "experiencers," to paraphrase Karel,[5] rather than as passive observers, who are on the receiving end of carefully orientated optics and privileged angles. When viewing an SEL film, audiences engage actively with reconfigured lived experience instead of passively receiving didactic information intent on "making a point." This filmmaking technique takes risks – among them, the possibility that viewers will react with dismissive impatience, frustration, boredom, or annoyance at the absence of explanatory signposting or expert analysis.

Lucien Castaing-Taylor

Lucien Castaing-Taylor studied anthropology, philosophy, and theology at Cambridge University in the UK as an undergraduate. After receiving his Bachelors of Arts, he left the UK to pursue an MFA at the University of Southern California's School of Cinema in the US. There, he studied with anthropologist Timothy Ash and subsequently pursued his Ph.D. in anthropology at the University of California, Berkeley. His first movie, *Made in the USA*, codirected with Ilisa Barbash, focuses on the use of child labor in Los Angeles' garment factories. His second movie, *In and Out of Africa*, also codirected with Ilisa Barbash, is a fairly conventional depiction of the circulation of material culture. Seventeen years later, Barbash and Castaing-Taylor codirected *Sweetgrass*, a film I will discuss later in this chapter in detail.

Finding contemporary writing about his film work and process by Castaing-Taylor is challenging, and what is available is mostly theoretically orientated monographs or journal articles (*Visualizing Theory*, "Iconophobia" 1996); analyses of other people's movies (*Robert Gardner* 2008); theses (*In and Out of Africa* 2004); instructional texts (*Cross-Cultural Filmmaking* 1997); editorial contributions (books on Robert Gardner and David MacDougall 2006); and director/artist statements. *POV Magazine* (2011), based in Toronto, Canada, wrote a detailed piece on the SEL, but during the interview process Castaing-Taylor remained elusive, steering the interviewer away to other conversations and past interviews with other active SEL ethnographic filmmakers.

It is my goal in this book to try to probe Castaing-Taylor's and other SEL filmmakers' films as examples of the kind of experiential video ethnography that this book seeks to describe and analyze. I have personally noted that Castaing-Taylor and Barbash's movies chronologically and progressively move away from the use of language, reflective interviews, and music, becoming less and less reliant on explicit signposting and discursive meaning making. In their early film *In and Out of Africa*, for example, much of the film's narrative is conveyed through verbal proposition, montage, and non-diegetic means. It is an ethnography that "speaks" with rhetorically expository tones, through didactic delivery of knowledge, and the provision of contextualizing verbal information that guides audiences' interpretation of the film's premise. Twenty years later, the film *Leviathan* is almost completely nonverbal: it barely contains an understandable spoken sentence. While words are used to clarify and explain internal thoughts and external situations in *In and Out of Africa*, *Leviathan* immerses audiences in an ethereal nonverbal environment. Audiences rely on synesthetic participation to work through the movie's multifaceted impressions.

One possible key to understanding Castaing-Taylor's aesthetic shift in his filmmaking over the past 20 years is to note a statement he has publicly made about his distrust of words. "I really don't like talking about the SEL," discloses Castaing-Taylor in an interview with Jay Kuehner.[6] "I don't trust myself. I have nothing to say. But to the extent that it's worth paying attention to at all, much better if folks like you do than we be allowed to propagandize ourselves." In person Castaing-Taylor shared a similar sentiment with me during the RIDM film festival in Montreal before a retrospective of the SEL projects: "I do not trust my words." In an email exchange with Irene Borger, head of the Herb Alpert Awards in the Arts, Castaing-Taylor remarked, "If I could say in words what I thought the work was, I wouldn't bother making it." Castaing-Taylor reiterated this sentiment in an interview with Scott MacDonald when asked if *Sweetgrass* is more concerned with sheep than with humans, to which Castaing-Taylor replied,

> Oh, I don't know. I don't trust anything I say about the film. The other day at a Q and A after a screening, I even found myself reciting something from a review as if it was my own take on the film! If we could say in words what the film ... is about, we wouldn't have had to make it.[7]

I believe that the SEL's commitment to an aesthetic grounded in fluid, ambiguous, and open-ended cinema is well expressed by Castaing-Taylor in this interview extract:

> Films, like anything that humans make, are always about something in some way. But to imagine that they are about something that could be expressed in words outside the fabric of the film itself is kind of ludicrous, 'cause then you wouldn't make the film, you'd write it. But fiction films in particular, narrative films, are not reducible to a point, or to making a statement about the world. And non-fiction documentary suffers by contrast with this burden that spectators put on it, that filmmakers put on it ... which is that it's always elaborating an argument about the world, it's reducible to making a statement about the world, it's usually a political or evaluative statement. And to imagine that the whole swath, the whole domain of reality, of everything that is non-fiction, is divested of its plenitude, of its richness, of the whole experiential sensory qualities of actually being in the world, of lived experience itself, so that they can be reduced to meaning, can be encapsulated in language, in prose, is such a travesty.[8]

I also note that Castaing-Taylor's films tend to emphasize the human voice and speech as sounds rather than as language formulations. Discussing *Sweetgrass*, Castaing-Taylor states,

> It's a film with not much spoken language. A lot of the spoken language that is included is spoken in fragments rather than in full sentences or with any kind of clarity. It's spoken indirectly to the other ranchers or as a soliloquy to the sheep. It's a lullaby, trying to bed them down at night,

rather than to some imagined, unseen TV audience. It's a different use of the spoken word, a limited one.[9]

I will now segue from the SEL's ideas about speech, language, and words in their films to a further set of ideas and practices centered around the idea of experiential immersion.

Methodological characteristic #1: experiential immersion

A methodological approach that distinguishes SEL films from cinema verité and direct cinema is the Lab's deliberate use of cinematic techniques that foster a sense of experiential immersion in the film as it plays out on screen. The most obvious example is the use of extended long-takes that build to a sense of culminating experience, so that the viewer seems to be experiencing the film's physical world in unfolding real time. This involves a feeling for audiences of enlarging and magnifying sensations, building on the continuity of the experience of the film's world rather than fragmenting it through cutting or montage. As Castaing-Taylor has written:

> Like Dewey the SEL is concerned, not to analyze, but to actively produce aesthetic experience, and of kinds that reflect and draw on but do not necessarily clarify or leave one with the illusion of "understanding" everyday experience, and it also seeks to transcend what is often considered the particular province of the human, and delve into nature ...[10]

Many contemporary documentary films are concerned to signpost and present to viewers the "meaning" of each scene by clarifying it with exposition. By contrast, SEL films often depict lived experience as a solitary piece or stand-alone vignette. SEL films deliberately refuse to clarify settings or setup and rarely give any kind of conventional narrative cue. The Lab's films often begin in the dark, with sound entering prior to the appearance of the image (see MacDonald 2013). The deliberate choice of putting audiences in a visually deprived, decontextualized environment involves asking audiences to work their way through disorientation; in other words, instead of relying on cues, titles, or words, audiences must actively use synesthetic knowledge, embodied responses, and proprioceptive skills to "make sense" of the film. In these ways audiences' own bodies and sense become involved in the sensemaking and interpretation of the film.

It's also worth noting that while SEL films may start in disorientating ways they are not vague but intensely material. Each film gradually builds a strong sense of place, immersively. Environments and objects in SEL films can sometimes seem to have agency and can act with sensory force. Gondolas, trawlers, sheep, construction sites, bodies practicing performances, parks, and recycling plants all come alive in vivid and extraordinary ways.

Many more conventional documentary films will establish the film's setting through establishing scenes that set up the film's location, place, or world, sometimes as a form of "B-roll" or even in an overhead or aerial shot. Many documentary films use quick shots to "fill in" or supply information in their storytelling: for example, a five-second establishing shot of a location or setting where the story will take place. SEL documentary films, by contrast, deliberately go inside the environment of the film, prioritizing the experientially immersive over the fragmented sound bite or pop-up explanatory, informational shots. Background sounds, such as a passing airplane, are usually removed as undesirable "noise" in more conventional documentary films, yet in SEL films are foregrounded as centers of attention in ways that produce strong physical experiences of noise, as part of an immersive, saturating approach to evoking the overall environment of the film.

In SEL films these immersive approaches to the environment make the viewing experience quite different to watching a more traditional documentary film. Eschewing voiceover, explanation, expository information, clarity of "establishing shots" or "B-roll" footage, editing for climax, plot, tension, or narrative stories, reflective on-the-spot or after-the-fact interviews, and diegetic music used to prompt a leading or singular interpretation, Castaing-Taylor elaborates on SEL's aesthetic approaches:

> … [The] works emerging from the SEL are more concerned with issues of aesthetics and form than documentary usually is, and are for the most part opposed to conventional documentary on a slew of counts: to the journalistic use of interviews, or of featuring subjects merely talking about their lives, ex post facto, rather than actually living them; to the reductive range of dramaturgical narrative structures documentary typically deploys, their linearity and predilection for resolution and closure; and to the narrow repertoire of styles that are sanctioned by the gatekeepers of documentary practice – in particular the ongoing hegemony half a century after the fact of a kind of lazy and lax cinéma vérité, and the consecration of a frequently unseeing and unsensing, putatively "observational," aesthetic within the ethnographic film world, and its dismissal of anything experimental, structurally rigorous, or stylistically demanding as provincially "avant-garde" or unduly self-reflexive or self-indulgent. It is as if the custodians of the sacred flame of ethnographic cinema are oblivious to any developments in art or in film since Jean Rouch's experiments in ethno-fiction in the 1960s and 1970s.[11]

Castaing-Taylor also acknowledges the influence of ideas concerning "wild" experience, presence, and expressiveness and, in a rare explanatory statement worth quoting at length, Castaing-Taylor comments on his interest in the idea of an experiential approach:

SCOTT MACDONALD: … Your interest in filmmaking seems experiential in the sense that John Dewey talks about artworks being concentrations/intensifications of lived experiences, rather than informational presentations and/or theoretical conjectures; and your sense of "ethnographic film" seems much broader than what that term traditionally is taken to mean.

CASTAING-TAYLOR: Well, you pretty much just said it all. Juxtaposing perspectives from the sciences, the arts, and the humanities, the aim of the Sensory Ethnography Lab is to support innovative combinations of aesthetics and ethnography, especially with work conducted through audiovisual media (video, sound, film, photography, and "new" hypermedia), that are at an angle to dominant conventions in anthropology, documentary, and art practice … As for situating the Sensory Ethnography Lab within the larger trajectories of visual anthropology, documentary, and contemporary art, your reference to Dewey seems right on. On the one hand, the SEL's ethnographic imperatives mean that the work coming out of it is generally more committed to the "real" than art is, especially conceptual and post-conceptual art, and to a form of expression that is somehow adequate to the magnitude of human experience. Or, if that's too much, at least to working within (as well as against) various species of realism. Dewey seems crucial here, especially *Art as Experience*, which has somehow been neglected by anthropologists of art. I would guess there are at least two reasons why. In the first place, Dewey takes as his subject, although he does not use the term, the phenomenology of aesthetic experience – experience that surely is at the heart of human existence if anything is, but which is something that anthropologists of art have actually not been very interested in, concerned instead to reduce being to mere meaning, and art to so many epiphenomena of one or another culture, to mere "material culture," or to something analogous to ritual, and so on and so forth.

In the second place, Dewey is deeply invested in "nature," to recursively coupling aesthetic experience not simply with everyday experience, but also with its infra-human animalic sources, and the at once sub- and supracutaneous interaction between what he called – three decades or more before the coinage of "cyborgs" – the co-constituting "live creature" and its "environment," whereas for social and cultural anthropologists talk of nature has long been something of an embarrassment – to be disavowed, immediately transformed into "second nature," mediated through-and-through by culture, a mere social construction, or (as with Bruno Latour) a dangerous political or scientific ideology to be actively combated.

Like Dewey, the SEL is concerned, not to analyze, but to actively produce aesthetic experience, and of kinds that reflect and draw on but do not necessarily clarify or leave one with the illusion of "understanding" everyday experience, and it also seeks to transcend what is often considered the particular province of the human, and delve into nature – in short, to re-conjugate culture with nature, to pursue promiscuities between animalic and non-animalic selves and others, and to restore us both to the domain of perception, in all its plenitude, rather than the academic game of what Dewey called "recognition," or of naming, that he derided as a barely conscious endeavor; and to the fleshy realm, in Merleau-Ponty's phrase, of "wild being," in which the invisible, far from being the negation or contradiction of the visible, is in fact its "secret sharer," its *membrure* … (MacDonald 2014, p. 400).

Methodological characteristic #2: reflexive presence of the ethnographer

Another influential figure in video ethnography, J.P. Sniadecki, who made several movies as a Ph.D. student in the SEL with Castaing-Taylor as his advisor, echoes Castaing-Taylor's ideas about experiential filmmaking and elaborates on his own presence, and subjectivity, stating:

> Again, I do not intend to misrepresent my filmmaking as somehow void of filmmaker perspective or subjectivity. For, no matter where directed, every act of pointing a camera carries the subjective imprint of the operator … Thus, even when fixed on a tripod, my camera in *Chaiqian (Demolition)* is *always embodied*, and the images it captures are "not just the images of other bodies; they are also images of the body behind the camera and its relation to the world" … To fail to include these questions and curiosities felt disingenuous, and by doing so I would be occluding not only a dimension of the filmmaking encounter but also insights into the film-subjects' (and my own) experiences of urban life, ephemeral relations, media representation, and technology that were instigated by the very act of filming.
>
> *Sniadecki 2014*

Acknowledging the presence of the filmmaker during filmmaking is usually referred to as a form of reflexivity. Reflexivity is the process of "contextualizing the content of a film by revealing aspects of its production" (MacDougall 2011 pp. 276–295). Examples of reflexivity include incorporating the voice of the filmmaker in a film or the movement of the camera, glances by subjects at the filmmaker, or how the filmmaker directs attention. SEL films tend to acknowledge the artifice of filmmaking by embracing reflexivity. For example, in *Sweetgrass*, characters verbally refer to and include Castaing-Taylor as part of the film in the following statements: "Lucien fell asleep" and "Bye, Lucien!" In *Foreign Parts*, Paravel and Sniadecki both speak, and Paravel is seen providing her cell phone to a woman in distress. In *Manakamana* and *People's Park*, characters are shown staring, watching, or glancing at the filmmakers as they make their film. In *Leviathan*, a fisherman sternly glares directly into the camera as he waits for his partner to return a bucket in which to place fish. In *Demolition*, workers talk about the filmmaker (in this case, Sniadecki), assuming he doesn't speak or understand their language. A performance artist taunts Julia Yezbick's camera in *Into the Hinterlands*, and a woman is shown dancing with the filmmakers in *Foreign Parts*. The implicit reflexivity of SEL films incorporates the

> stamp of the filmmaker's research interests and personal involvement. It can be read in a multitude of signs in how the film has been made, from the camerawork to the editing, to the responses of the people on the screen. It is an expression of the filmmaker's living presence in the film.
>
> *MacDougall 2011, p. 276–295*

Such reflexive moments allow audiences to witness how the filmmaker and characters are both methodologically indexed as sensing selves, visibly and sonically present rather than disguised through pretensions of erasure. When SEL filmmakers make themselves reflexively present to an audience, they reveal – through gestures – how the experience of making the film and of being present in a certain environment shapes them, how they in turn help shape the experience, and how they become part of the experience in their films – all of which are examples of reflexivity. The filmmaker, characters, and audience all share a unique position inside a common field of evoked experience.

A feature of these reflexive moments is that in SEL films audiences are aware of the filmmaker's body, and of the camera, functioning as sensing, tactile technology embedded within the environment of the film. In SEL films the embodied cameraperson deliberately aims to evoke immersive experience from within a particular situation or place, in order to be co-present with the environment and subjects. This situated co-presence echoes Merleau-Ponty's critique of essentialism.

> If we succeed in describing the access to the things themselves, it will only be through this opacity and this depth, which never cease: there is no thing fully observable, no inspection of the thing that would be without gaps and that would be total ... For a philosophy that is installed in pure vision, in the aerial view of the panorama, there can be no encounter with another: for the look dominates; it can only dominate things, and if it falls upon men it transforms them into puppets which move only by springs.
>
> *Merleau-Ponty 1965, p. 77*

In other words, SEL filmmakers do not attempt more than what is involved in co-presence; instead of trying to get "more," they focus on what is present, on residual traces, gesture, and all aesthetic experiences that emerge from being present. SEL films free audiences up to being present too; to immersive sensory experience. Immersion places audiences *inside* experiences through the senses. As Merleau-Ponty describes, the body is a "sensible sentient ... Where are we to put the limit between the body and the world, since the world is flesh? ... As flesh applied to a flesh the world neither surrounds it nor is surrounded by it ..." (Merleau-Ponty 1965, pp. 137–138).

Methodological characteristic #3: diegetic sound

> But what is it that makes one tune in to things like qualities of reverberation or timbre, or gravitate towards the weird sounds in music rather than melodies? Who knows? But later after I went to graduate school at the University of Chicago to look at different human approaches to living in the world, my long-standing interest in music and noise started to come into play there, and I started to wonder about how sound might function differently in different cultural situations.
>
> *Ernst Karel*[12]

As previously noted (MacDougall 2006, p. 273) in my discussion of the SEL's approach to the extended take, noise and sound are given a central, reverberating, resonant presence in SEL films and sounds tend to be prioritized over spoken language. The films' wide range of acoustic sounds and the SEL's aesthetic of an experiential approach to the duration and continuity of sound, these elements also correspond to Merleau-Ponty's and Dewey's writings on embodied being, prelinguistic sensory experience, and aesthetics. In SEL films, sound is given equal, or greater, emphasis than visual or perceptual fields of experience. SEL films immerse the body in an aural atmosphere through multiple textures of sounds. Aural cacophonies are offered up simultaneously: humming cicadas, walking feet, laughing children, recycling plastic, or musical gondolas. The aural environment of SEL films feels embodied and vital. SEL films' soundscapes pay attention to the sensuous sounds of humans, animals, and machines. Each SEL film's soundscape feels fully embodied, as well as defamiliarizing and often subtly grating on audiences' bodies in ways that activate and enliven sensory attention. Audiences' bodies are involved in responding to SEL films as sentient beings. Rather than operating as an explanatory, instrumental, or technical facet, an SEL soundscape feels "sonorous" in tone, with its free-form rhythms, sensuous cacophonies of environmental noises, and jarring styles that also incorporate distinctly musical and poetic qualities.

Indeed, each SEL film is carefully sound designed by Ernst Karel, who is credited as "sound designer" in all of the SEL's work. Karel's artistry makes the familiar sounds of an airplane, passing gondola, or bleats of sheep sound lyrical and unfamiliar. Sounds are presented in such a way that they sometimes seem sudden and unexpected, as though heard for the first time. Karel refers to sounds as "active experience" for audiences, and suggests that,

> experiencing [sounds] constitutes an intellectual challenge for the viewer, who must actively bring their critical faculties to bear on the experience

of the work, in effect to complete the work through their experience of it ... Where the experiential nature of certain kinds of strong ethnographic or documentary vilm [Karel's term for film/video] call for an active, exploratory response from their viewers, sound work asks even more of its audience.[13]

Karel's approach to sound, like so many aspects of the SEL body of film work, emphasizes the experiential. In an interview with *The Wire Salon* magazine, he states that,

> The practice of making nonfiction work which goes under the names media anthropology or sensory ethnography is based on the understanding that human meaning does not emerge only from language; it engages with the ways in which our sensory experience is pre- or non-linguistic, and part of our bodily being in the world. It takes advantage of the fact that our cognitive awareness – conscious as well as unconscious – consists of multiple strands of signification, woven of shifting fragments of imagery, sensation and malleable memory. Works of sensory media are capable of echoing or reflecting or embodying these kinds of multiple simultaneous strands of signification.[14]

Sounds reflect relationships formed during the recording and making of films and filmmakers – and sound designers like Karel – incorporate this reflexive process in a way that Karel refers to as "resonances" that become inseparable from encounters with experience. Karel quotes MacDougall:

> In his essay, "Visual anthropology and the ways of knowing," filmmaker David MacDougall writes of the "exploratory response demanded by visual works," or the principle of discovery at work in visual media, which is what calls on the experiencer to be an active participant in the work – the discovery of relationships between images, linked not only by their proximity but by their resonances ... This includes, for example, anthropologist Stephen Tyler's call for an evocation that "produces an understanding rather than an anthropological object" – a kind of understanding which is not separable from one's encounter with sensory experience, an understanding which is relational, which is experiential – and in which subject and object are bound up, never disengaged. The knowledge which is created remains part of the experience, and not a separate or separable object. Viewing documentary vilms, or listening to ethnographic audio, is less a matter of communicating information, per se, and more one of constructing new realities. These kinds of epistemological notions are key to our valuation of ethnographic audiovisual media today.[15]

By his own definition Karel's soundscapes can be considered as aesthetic knowledge in their own right, rather than as supplementary informational material accompanying the film. In SEL films, soundscapes form a central part of the film experience and the soundscape is often also deliberately open-ended in its interpretive possibilities.

Methodological characteristic #4: encounters

SEL films' emphasis on corporeal, sensuous experience and the Lab's films' aesthetic of avoiding obvious or explanatory "signposting" exposition tends to help foster ambiguity. For example, no one explains the meaning or story of the bells worn by the sheep in *Sweetgrass*. Instead, audiences simply listen to the sound of animals moving in a landscape, and experience the environment's sounds in the raw – bells, wind, bleats – as sheep stumble and get stuck in various textures underfoot: grit, snow, ice, trees, twigs, mud, and gravel. Through experiential understanding, using primarily sound, viewers develop a complex interpretive awareness of the sensuousness of the environment. They are bodily immersed inside encounters rather than verbally distanced by a narrator.

In these ways SEL filmmakers significantly break with the contemporary documentary mainstream, dominated by cinema verité and journalistic endeavors. Instead the SEL leads a movement toward, as Paravel explains, aesthetic encounters based on body-motion. Her efforts, she insists, are experimental, in the sense that she doesn't have a preconceived outcome of her film's story in advance. Paravel is also deliberate and tenacious in her aesthetic choices. Each motion she generates with the camera is a response to the motion she encounters. She moves with the motion of her subject matter, rather than directing it. Hearing and smelling are also central ways to interpret her environment. Contact, Paravel tells me, is important when becoming involved in the sensuousness around her. She attunes to an open-ended immersive connection between her and whatever environment she's recording. "My body takes in the surroundings and I pay attention to movement by listening to my body. It's a much more tactile experience. It is something I feel as I move" (personal interview 2011).

Paravel explains that her approach to *Foreign Parts* (codirected with Sniadecki) and *Leviathan* (codirected with Castaing-Taylor) was an "aesthetics of encounter." Each of these films involves lived experiences mutually shared by filmmakers and their subjects during the filmmaking process so that the films become the traces of these encounters. Paravel explains this process:

> every film is like an encounter … we don't have any dogma, we don't have any approach – nothing except our body and our willingness to do something. Though we do have a tendency to practice long-take shots where encounters occur inside the duration.[16]

Extended long-takes of unbroken duration, fluid in their movement and continuity, are a common characteristic of SEL films. Some shots can range anywhere from two (*Demolition*) to 80 (*People's Park*) continuous minutes in SEL films. As a means of prolonging aesthetic attention, long-take shots in SEL movies immerse audiences in extended sequences that help to change the audiences' experience of watching a film. Audiences are placed inside the experience through continuity in the presentation of spatiotemporal duration. In other words, because the duration of the extended sequence is unbroken from beginning to end, seamlessly occurring, each movement of the camera places the audiences in a different experiential position while minimizing the disruption of the continuity of space and time. SEL movies enlist audiences' senses by focusing on and enhancing sights and sounds in ways that defamiliarize the familiar. The creation of this interpretive space is largely achieved through use of the long-take, as described by MacDougall (2006). It is a technique that allows audiences sufficient time to adjust to viewing and interpreting a film using their bodily senses. Through this technique, audiences are able to encounter sensuous and aesthetic experience as a form of sensory knowledge that does not rely on language.

The depth of intimacy given to the immersive experience in SEL movies is somewhat unusual. It marks a shift away from the artificially constructed or arranged drama found in narratives that rely on the three-act structure with tension, conflict, and resolution between characters, the goal of which is to propel the narrative arc forward toward closure. The majority of SEL movies conclude in an open-ended way. In *Sweetgrass*, for instance, (John) drives away to an unknown destination. *Foreign Parts* never resolves the impending crisis of the planned New York Mets (Citibank) baseball park displacing the junkyard and its inhabitants. *Leviathan*'s final shot takes place inside complete darkness while the audience remains immersed in sound. *People's Park* concludes on an upbeat note of joyful revelry and celebratory dancing among cross-generations of people reverberating and gyrating to the sounds of music in a public park, formerly considered off-limits.

Conclusion: video ethnography as sensory knowledge

I believe that considering in detail the experiential and philosophical practices of the SEL discussed above can provide a valuable exercise in thinking about how the SEL's aesthetic approach to crafting sensory knowledge pushes the boundaries of ethnography's methodological limits. The SEL's synthesis of aesthetics and experience transforms what is usually termed "knowledge" in ethnography. The SEL's unique approach to experiential ethnography – derived from theories discussed in the previous chapter – moves beyond long-established notions of what is accepted or of what "counts" as ethnographic scholarship. No longer reliant on the spoken word, written, or textual accounts, video ethnography such as the SEL's ushers in new approaches to the foundations of how sensory knowledge is produced. The SEL approaches described in this chapter de-emphasize *representation* and *resemblance* in favor of harnessing *estrangement* and *expressionism*.

Video ethnography tends to do more than to simply offer audiences an interpretive space through which to explore new surroundings; it also allows audiences to experience familiar surroundings in ways that defamiliarize. I conclude with two main SEL contributions to the field of contemporary video ethnography.

First, SEL's methodological strength is to create an aesthetic experience by mediating or evoking a designated lived experience within a distinct environment or ecology of sights and sounds. The SEL's approach to video ethnography allows audiences to affectively see, hear, and feel a familiar environment in new and highly sensuous ways, therefore gaining a more complex and sensory interpretive understanding than could be gleaned from reading about such an environment. In other words, SEL films allow audiences to experience places through heightened sensory exploration. SEL films prioritize sensory saturation because they deliberately do not provide exposition or explanation of what is actually "going on" in the film, thereby avoiding narrowing meaning to a propositional argument or making a point, permitting different forms of sensory-based interpretive understanding.

Second, SEL's methodology tends to promote sensory-based understanding of how human and nonhuman life are merged. Thanks to the SEL's approach to aesthetic evocation of lived experience, video ethnography becomes capable of evoking invisible or hidden aspects of the social world, including the nonhuman or more-than-human and the nonverbal or nonlanguage based. Through prioritizing sensory knowledge over explanatory or rhetorical language, audiences are invited into a space in which they are free to interpret meaning and also to challenge it and hierarchies of sense. Audiences are able to see familiar surroundings in unfamiliar ways, allowing for a more complex understanding of the social world.

To conclude, video ethnography is not merely a novel way of presenting traditional research, it is a methodological sensibility that allows aspects of the social world previously neglected or omitted from research to be experienced and considered. As a form of sensory scholarship, video ethnography is capable of generating a wider and fuller understanding of the social world, and breaks away from traditional limitations imposed by conventional representational ethnography.

Notes

1　http://sel.fas.harvard.edu/.
2　https://sel.fas.harvard.edu/.
3　https://earroom.wordpress.com/2013/02/14/ernst-karel/.
4　http://povmagazine.com/articles/view/sense-and-sensibility-harvards-sensory-ethnography-lab.
5　https://earroom.wordpress.com/2013/02/14/ernst-karel/.
6　www.fandor.com/keyframe/savage-in-a-sense.
7　https://herbalpertawards.org/artist/beyond-words.
8　www.fandor.com/keyframe/savage-in-a-sense.
9　http://archive.pov.org/sweetgrass/interview/.

10 www.frameworkonline.com/festivals/nyff2012/sweetgrass-ilisa-barbash-and-lucien-castaing-taylor.html.
11 www.frameworknow.com/#!con-ruminating-on-sweetgrass/c5jt.
12 https://earroom.wordpress.com/2013/02/14/ernst-karel/.
13 http://earroom.wordpress.com/2013/02/14/ernst-karel/.
14 http://earroom.wordpress.com/2013/02/14/ernst-karel/.
15 http://earroom.wordpress.com/2013/02/14/ernst-karel/.
16 www.indiewire.com/2013/03/lost-at-sea-the-morbid-fascinations-of-fishing-doc-leviathan-40510/.

3

SWEETGRASS AND *LEVIATHAN*

Case studies in video ethnography

The previous chapter explored the theoretical precursors to and philosophical influences of the Sensory Ethnography Lab (SEL) and concluded with an outline of four central methodological techniques emerging from the SEL: experiential immersion, reflexive presence, diegetic sound, and encounters. This chapter examines these characteristics in more depth by focusing on the craft behind two well-acclaimed movies from the SEL, *Sweetgrass*, co-directed by Castaing-Taylor and Ilisa Barbash, and Leviathan, co-directed by Castaing-Taylor and Véréna Paravel. Through extensive interviews with the co-directors, and by analyzing *Sweetgrass* and *Leviathan*, I will examine both films' methodological techniques to demonstrate how they are edited and constructed within specific philosophical principles identified in previous chapters.

Sweetgrass: a case study

The opening shot in *Sweetgrass* is of a single sheep grazing and chewing cud while wearing a bell on a mountainous plain. For a moment the sheep is filmed unobtrusively in traditional observational style. Moment after moment, however, the observational point of view fluidly shifts as the sheep slowly turns its head, stops chewing, and stares directly into the lens of the camera – looking directly at the audience, fixed and frozen – staring with focused intention. It's as though the film is commenting self-reflexively: the audience and movie are part of a shared experience. This single shot signals a departure from observational film-making practices in ethnography.

Experiential movies make us aware of ourselves as both subject and object; we sense ourselves as the watching audience anticipated by the movie. As a result we become more aware of ourselves in relation to the act of watching as well as in relation to others. In the gap between ourselves and the sheep in *Sweetgrass* we, as the film's audience, immersively become aware of ourselves through the gaze of the other. A suggestive quote from Merleau-Ponty underscores this feeling:

> Whereas the other's gaze … envelops me wholly … it is the entry on the scene of someone else. I do not simply feel myself frozen, I am frozen by a look, and if it were for example an animal that looked at me, I would know only a feeble echo of this experience … I am wholly implicated … in this perception that takes possession of me.
>
> *Merleau-Ponty 1965, p. 72*

From its opening scene, *Sweetgrass* invites audiences into a synesthetic immersion into an ecosystem in which humans are invested in animals and animals are invested in humans. *Sweetgrass* uses the extended takes so that sight and sound combine to form an immersive reality experienced through the film's particular, slow, intense aesthetic. The real, the filmmakers insist, is not something "represented," but something "aimed for." Lucien Castaing-Taylor, shortly after making *Sweetgrass*, suggests that, "Very little cinema seems to aspire to resituate the human in this larger swat of nature to which we inescapably belong."[1] The following interview regarding the editing of *Sweetgrass* and Castaing-Taylor's response help illuminate the film's ambience.

CINEMA SCOPE: The notion of corporeal engagement is registered acutely. Not only are you as a documentarian compelled to become more physically engaged, albeit under less obligation, but you are witness to a simple but arduous routine of labour. The toll is reflected particularly in John, in the weary tone of his voice and the weathered lines of his face. There's such contrast between the two sheepherders, John and Pat: One tender and affectionate, riding low in his saddle, the other broken, practically misogynistic, and bitching. There's something elegiacally cowboy though, a sense of the mythic West, the frontier. John is humming old cowboy tunes and they live in tents and light fires. There are even Indians, counting the faintest trace of arrowheads, which is a painful historic irony, merely a diversion for the cowboys.

CASTAING-TAYLOR: In terms of the contrasting characters I think it's an illusion, a function of the editing, unfortunately, because any film is reductive, a palimpsest of reality. We definitely intended there to be a tension between intimacy and violence, eroticism and misogyny, tenderness and aggression – all of these things being part and parcel of the fabric of our lives, of human existence, and definitely our relationship to other animals. That's universal. But I see now how the film perpetuates a simplistic schema of the serene, laconic elder – John could be so loquacious and sweet with the sheep, but he pretty much clams up with humans – versus the younger man, pushed to his limits, who goes off on this bestial, logorrheic diatribe. But I totally adore the interspecies promiscuity of his rant, how in a split second he manages to morph the sheep in his charge into pigs, whores, darlings, girly girls, bitches, goat-climbing cocksucking motherfuckers.[2]

I would go further to suggest that the editing of spoken language in *Sweetgrass* is deliberately obfuscating, leaving words unintelligible, incomplete, difficult to decipher, and riddled with poetic, musical cursing that verges on theatrical performance. The first human voice to appear in *Sweetgrass* is an English slang word so arcane that it does not even appear in an English dictionary: "kumbaday." According to Castaing-Taylor, the word is a contraction of "Come, I bid thee!" The editing of *Sweetgrass* is not intended to clarify. The film doesn't use discursive language that speaks as voice-over or directly to the camera to clarify or explain what is happening. Instead, the sonic editing in *Sweetgrass* distorts sounds and defamiliarizes sound to create deliberate aesthetic muddling between beast, human, and us, the audience. Castaing-Taylor explains this editing process:

> But the important thing is the affect, the emotion, the corporeal experience. It's not about a verbal transcript. It's more about at once the bestiality and the musicality of language than what is being intentionally "communicated" in some discursive sense. Our interest was skewed toward the affective colouration and the embodied engagement with the world rather than with understanding every word.[3]

The experience of *Sweetgrass* puts the audience in a position in which they are barely able to understand spoken words, much as the ranchers in the movie are barely able to hear each other or communication. Failed attempts to communicate are experienced in the middle of a cacophony of noisy sheep and bellowing humans who yell to each other, as they try to steer their horses using gestures inside a hubbub of chaotic sound while delivering *interminable verbal* instructions through walkie-talkies amidst 3,000 bleating sheep surrounded by dust, dirt, and barking dogs. Yet, through careful editing, none of what is spoken is clear in this context of unruly animals and bewildered herders. Hence the experiential confusion is conveyed wholesale. The befuddlement, I suggest, is a deliberate editing technique that accentuates confusion rather than tries to clarify it, as a way of "harvesting" the experience of indecipherable speech comingled with competing background noise, all part of the environmental harshness of the film as a sensory experience, in which dialogue remains opaque and mixed in with gritty, grunting sounds. This editing style is very much a reflection of Dewey's notion of choosing to mediate embodied aesthetic experience, however bestial, muddy, or chaotic, in order to be faithful to the raw experience, instead of seeking to "clean it up" through a more picturesque and organized representation of pastoral life.

Castaing-Taylor explains this aesthetic approach in his written statement on the making of *Sweetgrass*.

As we began work on the film, I returned to Wordsworth, and when re-reading *Michael* I realised he was anything but the unfettered romanticist I remembered him as. Until Wordsworth, the whole pastoral tradition, from Theocritus and Virgil, through Petrarch and Garcilaso, to Marot and Spenser – had idealised and allegorised shepherds out of bodily existence. Where would you ever encounter a shepherd snoring, peeing or cursing the loneliness or drudgery of the work?[4]

Castaing-Taylor's references to "peeing" in documentaries is clearly influenced by David MacDougall and Robert Gardner who referenced these bodily discharges in 2006: "Robert Gardner observes that fiction films, despite their frequent claims to realism, 'never show anything as ordinary or as innocent as someone taking a pee'" (MacDougall 2006, p. 20). Perhaps it's evident that Castaing-Taylor and Barbash included the peeing scene in *Sweetgrass* as an homage or nod to both MacDougall and Gardner.

Castaing-Taylor continues his philosophical stance along a similar line of thought in a recorded statement on his editing approach. Here he directly mentions Dewey.

With *Sweetgrass*, we transposed the genre to the American West, where we sought to convey at once the allure and the ambivalence of the pastoral. We tried to give a sense of what it is like to spend months at a time alone in the mountains with 3,000 sheep in one's charge. We also – as preposterous as it may sound – tried to evoke what it was like to be one of those charges, to be a sheep in an impossibly large band herded up to 11,000 feet the moment the snow melts, and down again as autumn approaches. In a sense our film bestializes the humans, as John Dewey argued all art should, recoupling our humanity with our base animalism (something to which we seem increasingly oblivious). But we also subjectify and at times anthropomorphize the sheep.[5]

Similarly, during an interview with Brandon Harris of *Filmmaker Magazine*, Castaing-Taylor comments on his efforts to preserve, through editing choices, this feeling of the immense experiential labor of *Sweetgrass*.

[T]he way they cuss, the way they snore, the way they pee, the way they live their lives is super real. The way all of our lives are, the way George Bush and Barack Obama's lives are, but typically documentary subjects, when they are in front of the camera, want to put on their Sunday best and dress up, act up. They are performing in an idealized version of themselves. We were interested in the nitty gritty, the difficulty of life as it's lived, and the difficulty of these people's lives, of cowboys lives, of shepherds lives. When we look at the whole history of the pastoral, the poetry from the classics onward, of painting, of the pastoral as a genre within mythology and literature, within cinema too, such as *Nanook of the North* for example, you get so little sense of what immense amount of labor is involved in a day of a shepherd's life, what its actually like to inhabit the body of a shepherd rather than the bourgeois consumer representation of some idealized relationship to nature.[6]

Experiential editing

I have thus far discussed how choosing to record and edit to convey directly lived experience means choosing to omit signposting, or propositional prose – clear verbal articulations, titles, explanations, and exposition. But this doesn't mean there is any less editing work or effort in *Sweetgrass*, or that the film simply depicts without shaping through careful editing choices. On close analysis editing choices in *Sweetgrass* deliberately seek to evoke sensuous knowledge, or experience, by editing in order to accentuate acoustic musical qualities and to emphasize visuals that touch audiences through their senses. For example, layers of diverse sheep sounds blend with weather sounds and the blustery audio of the film's *lieux* to produce a specific and intended affect. Experiential editing prioritizes the soundtrack of the environment as well as the diagetic sounds of human technology such as cell phones, walkie-talkies, and creaking saddles. Castaing-Taylor comments on this process.

> The real stars here, however, are the sheep. Very little time goes by without hearing the ever present bleating of the flock, moving in unison over the grassy Montana landscapes. The natural sound of the wilderness provides its own soundtrack, and the filmmakers wisely don't add any other musical accompaniment. The silences are as powerful as any great monologue. This isn't a Hollywood romanticized vision of the Old West, but the romance is still inherent. Even as we see these modern day cowboys cursing a blue streak into their cell phones or communicating with each other via walkie-talkies, there's still something intrinsically romantic about heading into the wild frontier on horseback, and living off the land. *Sweetgrass* is, above all, a chronicle of the last sheep drive, the end of an era, the death of a way of life, and the closing of a chapter of American history. Its unassuming beauty makes for a quietly engrossing ode the shimmering mystique of the West, and it captures the landscape's timeless, enduring appeal, while offering a time capsule of a poignant moment in American history.[7]

Sweetgrass viscerally places viewers in remote places where they experience the sensory disorientation of an unpredictable, wild environment. Disorientating sounds, images, dust, and wilderness blend with domesticated sheep. The soundscape and landscape, in all its gritty ruggedness, is edited much as the inarticulate humans in the movie communicate. Its untamed cliffs, jutting rocks, dusty fields, snow-capped mountains, ice on mud – all are as rugged as the characters' bodies and befuddled speech patterns. Landscapes, animals, humans, and the elements are edited to evoke the raw experience of existing in the wild, accentuated by the sound of 3,000 sheep bawling, grazing, and jostling as the ranchers struggle to direct them to desired locations. Nothing is signposted or explained. This experiential approach to editing immerses viewers in the plentitudes of sensuous experience and avoids all the redundancies and platitudes of explanatory language overlay.

Castaing-Taylor and Barbash edit *Sweetgrass* to prioritize the presence of the vast herd, the ranch herders, and the landscape to evoke their exterior phenomenological life worlds. Indeed, in an interview in *Cinema Scope*, Castaing-Taylor refers to the editing approach of "evoking," much as referenced by Vannini (2015a) and Merleau-Ponty's notion of "brute" experience:

> We ended up trying to be more phenomenological, you could say: evoking the lifeworld of the sheepherders as best we could, and to let that speak for itself, without any overt editorializing on our part. But not just the sheepherders – also the sheep, and especially the place itself. It's out of fashion to see nature as anything other than some secondary cultural construction, but we're all part of it, as much as city folks suppose otherwise, and throughout history humans and animals have commingled in ways that have deeply affected the kinds of beings we've become. But what phenomenologist ever considers the lifeworld of an animal? It'd be a joke. Yet at the same time, how can you not? … But when you're with them, and especially day in day out in such close quarters up in the mountains, their allegorization just falls away, and you're left encountering brute sheep, negotiating with them where to go, where to bed down, where to feed, whatever: you're in this embodied relationship, resisting, cajoling, cohabiting together. In many ways, the sheep stole *Sweetgrass'* thunder, and I think we probably ended up doing a better job portraying their experience of their world than we did of the humans'.[8]

Speaking to Megan Ratner (2010, p. 24) in *Film Quarterly*, Castaing-Taylor and Barbash invoke experiential editing by highlighting the camera angles in the final cut meant to "evoke the experiences of the sheep, of what it was like to inhabit their bodies, rather than to stare at them as objective bodies/ animals." The editing emphasis encouraged viewers to "bear witness to people (and animals) actually living their lives" (Ratner 2010, p. 24). One outcome of this approach is the production of sensuous knowledge, or, in other words, the delivery of a range of unusual choreographic perspectives, for example: showing and hearing the sheep's moving hooves; recording sheep from their vantage point by placing the camera from behind their rear ends as they bellow and grunt (during the Sheep-wreck scene, for instance);

holding long duration shots that allow kinetic and aesthetic aspects to unfold in real time; and skillfully conveying grating physical and sound textures that situate viewers within the immediacy of sensuous, perceptive phenomena. As Ratner explains,

> the camerawork shadows the subjects, more concerned with getting the feel for what the cowboys are doing than for clarifying everything for the viewer. *Sweetgrass* leaves much unexplained; yet though you feel slightly out of your depth, there is never a sense of confusion. It's an approach that honors the skilled work on display.
>
> *Ratner 2010, p. 25*

While editing *Sweetgrass*, Castaing-Taylor and Barbash chose to both juxtapose and enmesh the human and nonhuman. They also chose to contrast the inanimate stark hostile physical environment with the mammalian warmth and neediness of animated animal and human sounds, and offset soundscape with movement and action. The consequence is that landscape, animals, and humans are all actors. Sheep look back, speak, talk, communicate, act, perform, disrupt, die, and so on. In other words, sheep *act or perform* activities, as active participants in the co-construction of the film's dramatic environment rather than as passive objects over which viewers exert visual control. There is also the issue of direction: the sheepherders attempt to direct the animals in desired directions. Thus, a deliberate editing choice is to emphasize tension that exists between what sheep do as they drift off course, and what humans want them to do. To paraphrase Merleau-Ponty, the sheep are sensible and sentient, subject and object, flesh of flesh. Their animal bodies carry them toward an end point, but the film remains ambiguous or inconclusive about the power relations of this animal–human relationship, leaving the question unanswered: could the sheep arrive at their own destination without the assistance and direction of humans? The editing choice to emphasize *ambiguous* experience over logocentric clarity pits the rugged, physical terrain against the natural movements of the sheep's' bodies. It also raises the issue of how this *ethnographic* perspective of evoking ambiguity has proven to be problematic for traditional ethnographic film festival programming.

CINEMA SCOPE: So would you describe *Sweetgrass* as a work of visual anthropology?
CASTAING-TAYLOR: You should call it whatever you want to call it. Every ethnographic film festival has rejected it summarily. Ambiguity, or any kind of aesthetic opacity that isn't readily translatable into the limpid clarity of expository prose, is somehow lacking for anthropologists, in their quest for "cultural meaning", which they're hell-bent on linguifying. And as often as not, out of all recognition. Clarity for me is an illusion, a product of a certain kind of cultural textology. I'm never clear about anything; are you? Isn't cognitive and sensory muddle the human condition? I'm not desperate for

Sweetgrass to be recuperated as a work of visual anthropology, but simply because it doesn't tell you what it's about, and because there aren't that many words in it, doesn't for me mean it isn't a work of anthropology. It actually feels profoundly so to me, but maybe a more philosophical anthropology. And if I'm to take your question precisely – is the film "anthropo-logy"? – I guess I would say that *Sweetgrass* tries to relativise both the anthropos and its logos.

CINEMA SCOPE: And it's not pedagogical per se, as the line of inquiry is experiential. Is this why you call yourself a recordist as opposed to director?

CASTAING-TAYLOR: It goes back to this notion of our investment in the empirical, and synch sound. For instance, we never asked anybody to do anything. With the camera, I tried to insinuate myself into a position of insignificance, so I wasn't affecting what was going on in front of the camera, but I also didn't want anyone to pretend I wasn't there. So to say I was "directing" is misleading. I prefer "registered by" but it's too machine-like! "Realized by" sounds OK in French, but it's risible in English. Recorded by is more humble, which seems only appropriate. We've actually never discussed it, but I've noticed that a lot of the people making work in Harvard's Sensory Ethnography Lab are opting for "recorded by" ... There's a way in which nonfiction films seek to appropriate the prestige of fiction with the whole "directed by" business, which is another reason to drop it.[9]

Experiential sound

In the making of *Sweetgrass*, Castaing-Taylor placed microphones on sheep, dogs, horses, and people as a way to evoke the experiential immediacy of "being there" from all perspectives. This recording choice generated a rich immersion in different audio worlds, demonstrating a particularly tactile use of sound, a sense in which sound is tied into subjects' movement, and the use of sound to immerse audiences into indexical and diegetic participation in the world of the film through sensuous synesthetic experience. The editing style here once again is to emphasize the experiential and immediate characteristics of life lived by the characters in the film. However, crucial here is the editing of sound during the process of shooting or recording the footage. Editing choices were made before, during, and after production. Castaing-Taylor explains this choice to Kuehner during an interview:

> I think this goes back to the difference between fiction and documentary. In traditional fiction films you're immersed in the diegesis, just as in post-Rabelaisian novels, there's this naturalistic sense of being there with the characters, which documentaries don't push as far as they might. With *Sweetgrass*, we try to give you a sense of almost synaesthetic participation, and a lot of that comes from the sound, and from working with wireless lavs. The

first year we used only four, listening to them up to a mile-and-a-half away. The second year I had eight. Mostly I put them on people, but occasionally I'd mic [put a microphone on] a horse, a dog, or a sheep. I couldn't afford to do that as much as I'd have liked. While recording with headphones, if I had two sound sources, one in my left ear, one my right, they could be up to three miles apart, and if I could get a good quality signal, it was incredibly interesting, and at times the synchronicities were completely surreal.[10]

A main difference between the experiential recording and editing style Castaing-Taylor describes above and the editing of most documentaries, is that most documentaries cut out or delete obtuse sounds as if they don't "add to the story" or fail to add clarity (or, interfere with the story). Additionally, editors will also sometimes add subtitles as a way to clarify muddled conversations. *Sweetgrass*, by contrast, is happy to merge sheep and human sounds to imply their corporeal coexistent shared experience. The editing choice of coupling diegetic sounds (animal and human), layered with a method of extended long-takes, situates viewers in an embodied, unfolding state of tension in relationships between sheep, ranchers, and the work the film depicts. Castaing-Taylor refers to this methodological and editing choice to Jay Kuehner during an interview with *Cinema Scope*.

> But the important thing is the affect, the emotion, the corporeal experience. It's not about a verbal transcript. It's more about at once the bestiality and the musicality of language than what is being intentionally "communicated" in some discursive sense. Our interest was skewed toward the affective colouration and the embodied engagement with the world rather than with understanding every word. That was also a political choice. Some people – educated urban middle-class non-Westerners – said we should subtitle the film, but there's something about people not being able to fully understand others that makes a statement about a culture that is not completely transparent or accessible. What gives them the right to understand them?[11]

The duration of shots is a part of this approach, or, in other words, how long the editing holds a shot. Shot length in *Sweetgrass* ranges from 20 seconds to two minutes and 20 seconds, an unusual degree of variation for any documentary film. Most nonfiction documentaries edit shots for about five seconds. Most documentary films also use "B-roll" to "cover" voice-over. Sometimes images are brought into the edit to literally illustrate what the spoken words state out loud. For example, if someone in the film is discussing fishing, the film might show fishing scenes. *Sweetgrass*, by contrast, edits diegetic sound without the presence of a spoken signifier and signified. Castaing-Taylor has staked out a rather rigorous editing stance in this decision to sync voice with image:

There was this temptation to move the sound around in the interests of the rhythms, in the interests of cinema and "art." But I'm a complete vulgar positivist about this. I wanted it to be ambiguous, whether it was a voice that was laid over or found within. It was empirically crude, but it matters to me in terms of documentary practice.[12]

Another notable editing absence is the conscious omission of a narrative construction that develops around desire, plots, and resolution. One gleans only a minimal narrative arc in the film's presentation: how the ranchers take 3,000 sheep up a mountain, over and through a mountain, and down a mountain. But it is what happens during this experience that provides the story of *Sweetgrass*. The editing choice to omit narrative plot, according to a director's statement written by Castaing-Taylor, was chosen to emphasize "being-there," or thick sensuous description.

We resolved to give as authentic a sense as we could of what it was like to spend months at a time alone with 3,000 sheep in your charge high in the mountains. We also – preposterously perhaps – tried to evoke what it was like to be one of those charges, to be a sheep in an impossibly large band herded up to 11,000 ft the moment the snow melts, and down again just as autumn approaches. In a sense, we bestialise the humans and subjectify and at times anthropomorphise the sheep.[13]

By analyzing the methodological and editing choices made in *Sweetgrass* we find that the construction of experiential video ethnographies, in both sound and visual, is not about clarifying or holding a mirror to reflect accurate translations of lived experience. Instead, experiential video ethnographies emphasize messiness and lack of clarity, the embodied and sonorous situations that transpire through encounters. Evoking these ambiguous situations of tension is partially done in the recording and filming process and partially through skilled, thoughtful editing in the postproduction phase, editing that consciously pays attention to aesthetic experience. The sensibilities involved in this kind of editing prioritize immersive embodiment and the sensuousness of contact rather than narrative clarity, linguistic contextualization, or signposting. Finally, the editing of *Sweetgrass* was explicitly and consciously influenced by Merleau-Ponty's approaches and the corporeal animism of John Dewey as I have shown, by citing a series of revealing interviews with Castaing-Taylor. Next, I turn my attention to *Leviathan* in order to further elaborate on the experiential concepts of immersion, reflexive presence, diegetic sounds, and encounters in a different yet intimately related film by Castaing-Taylor and Paravel.

Leviathan

Unlike the commitment to the temporal linearity and goal-orientated objective of herding sheep to a specific destination of *Sweetgrass, Leviathan*, set at sea, is devoid of temporal and spatial orientation and, at times, devoid of any sense of bearings at all. Its boldly embodied immersion into corporeal bodies – human and nonhuman is spectacular – suggesting a hallucinatory and cosmic gesture. Artistically and methodologically, *Leviathan* revels in evoking the real as other wordly. Stylistically, its methodological and cinematography technique paints a dirty and grainy perception of opaqueness amidst the kind of underwater darkness that subsumes light. At times, *Leviathan* verges on Vertov's montage and Brakhage's avant-garde painterly scratch; while at other times its seamless editing and temporal cinematography of dedicated durational long-takes evokes Bazinian unbroken extended sequences. It stylistically pronounces itself a groundbreaking work in its distinctive approach to recording and editing lived experience.

Questions of whether or not the film is empirical or artistic, anthropological or ethnographic feel quite irrelevant to the experience of *Leviathan*. *Leviathan* itself disregards such categorizations; freely merging ethnography with cinematic sweep. It is an experiential film that breaks with contemporary documentary conventions in many ways. Yet, *Leviathan* is also a mimetic project, refracting from intricate lived experiences in non-observational ways. *Leviathan* does more than immerse audiences, it submerges them, sinks them into experiences while in the middle of the ocean. As the cliché goes, the only way out is to work one's way through the experience. As Castaing-Taylor explains, "it's an 87-minute experience of being at sea, both metaphorically and literally."[14]

Leviathan's use of verbal or spoken language, unlike *Sweetgrass*, is minimal. Nothing spoken in the movie is coherent; speech is lost, drowned out by drone mechanical sounds that encapsulate the embodied experience of the fishermen. Evocative gestures and camera motion stand in as ways to evoke what Dewey calls "half-knowledge." The film's editing emphasizes corporeal movements and listening; it foregrounds how fishermen gesture to each other within a distinctive world of fish, ocean, metal, knives, blood, birds, and taking showers aboard their boat at sea. The film's editing portrays the fishing vessel as an actant – it is alive, ravishing, consuming, and eating everything in its path. Its indifference to nature devours, destroys, and disregards anything living or dead in its way, leaving behind phantasms lost at sea. The editing of *Leviathan* assembles cosmic images that plunge viewers into the sky, ghostly images of life ripped apart, floating underwater as traces of former life, decimated in a cosmic atmosphere. Deleuze refers to these cosmic and ghostly images as "recollection-images." "Those floating, dreamlike images that cannot be assigned a connection to history" (Marks 2000, p. 37). *Leviathan* is edited to avoid making any point. Castaing-Taylor vehemently elaborates on this editing choice.

> Question from audience: "What does the film say about the commercialization of fishing?"

CASTAING-TAYLOR: Nothing. We are not trying to say anything. But one thing we're trying to do is to make films that don't say anything. Films, like everything humans make, are always about something in some way. But to imagine that they are about something that could be expressed in words, outside of the fabric of the film itself, is kind of ludicrous, because then you wouldn't make the film, you would write it. But fiction films in particular, narrative films, are not reducible to a point, or to making a statement about the world. And non-fiction, documentary, suffers by contrast, with this burden that spectators put on it, that filmmakers put on it, that programmers put on it … which is always elaborating an argument about the world, it is reducible to making a statement about the world (it's usually a political or a value-added statement). And to imagine that the whole swat, that whole domain of reality, of everything that is non-fiction, is divested of its plenitude, of its richness, of the all experiential, sensory quality of actually being in the world, of lived experience itself, so that could be reduced to "meaning", encapsulated in language, in prose … That is such a travesty for those kind of films, which is why so many documentaries are so weak.[15]

The fishing vessel in *Leviathan* is a sensible sentient. Boats are often assumed to be inert and passive, yet the metal vessel in *Leviathan* is filmed to suggest that it breathes, eats, vomits, gurgles, and digests. It is alive in animistic ways. While it is alive, men are sometimes mechanical: shucking shellfish and slicing through flounder with mechanical speed. The vessel has spontaneous powers as a sensible living entity that astonishes and incites awe in its brute force and wild being. It is evoked as a thing with machinic (mechanical) sensibilities, something eminently magical in its astonishing power to destroy and act against all reason. The vessel has a will and acts with sensual force. In short, it is edited to evoke the experience of an experience, to paraphrase Sobchack (1992). Castaing-Taylor comments on Dewey's notion of "an experience of an experience."

CASTAING-TAYLOR: I'd say it's both easier and harder to try to simply give shape, to give form to an amorphous mass of aesthetic experience. The idea of making a documentary that provides an interpretation of the world is a very peculiar notion if you think about it. It's very odd if documentaries are claiming to have some privileged purchase on reality, on lived experience. Our desire was simply to give an experience of an experience.[16]

Leviathan, through its total immersion, invites its viewers to smell, feel, hear, taste, and perceive the experiences on the vessel from various dizzying locations. Viewers of the movie report seasickness, throwing up, dizziness, disorientation, flashes of lights, tasting and smelling of fish. "It's about interspecies and relationships," Paravel qualifies. "At some point we say interspecies bestiality, and the threshold between animal, human, and machine and the matter of the world in some totalizing way." Castaing-Taylor adds,

It's about bringing things together in a cosmic way … We weren't oblivious to the Thomas Hobbes reference, of course. Hobbes placed a lot of importance on the social contract and the state. He placed a lot of importance on the primary sense experience. So in a way we're at the other end of the spectrum. This film is immersive and first person and experiential, but there's no explanatory apparatus. The state and multi-nationals have played a huge role in commercial fishing over the last 150 years and we wanted to encourage people to think about their role in this process.[17]

Castaing-Taylor and Paravel juxtapose barely recognizable abstract images and sounds with deliberately defamiliarized images and sounds of familiar, everyday ocean-related phenomena such as fish, wires, boats, and salt water, overlapping the two in ways that are manifestly phenomenological and synesthetic in their editing choices and orientation. This approach to evoking lived experience pri-oritizes prelinguistic and embodied gestures. *Leviathan* introduces and takes ser-iously notions of ghostly haunting and cosmology as gestures of ethnographic lived experience. "It's about bringing things together in a cosmic way," Casta-ing-Taylor adds.[18]

Castaing-Taylor and Paravel's editing, I contend, is an attempt to make sense of their own personal transformation while making their film. They subjectivize the movie and transmogrify their experience by bringing viewers into what they experienced in the process of filming, and how they perceived their changing experience through their embodied encounters. The hallucinations experienced by viewers are the hallucinations and out-of-body, ghostly experiences that Cas-taing-Taylor and Paravel experienced, crafted to convey their own subjectivity as part of the shared encounter. They bring flesh and blood – embodiment – to cosmic forces, half-knowledge through a sensory or synesthetic multilayering.

The images we perceive and sounds we hear in *Leviathan* are more or less haptic (Marks 2000), but fragmentary and not altogether discernable; the sensory debris of coming in and out of consciousness, as though from a shipwreck. In the film we witness a disoriented bird that has lost its ability to navigate through physical damage, as it desperately attempts to orientate its way out of the metal vessel. Likewise, *Leviathan* is edited in ways that suggest losing consciousness – or rather, consciousness and intention are stripped bare to reveal a precognitive journey through immersive experiences during a liminal phase of being half awake, half asleep. *Leviathan* is a disoriented orientation. The compass is broken, gravity suspended, the world is turned upside down. *Leviathan* amplifies the rich-ness of this queasy hazy experience without reducing it to a referent. It adheres to Dewey's idea that language emaciates experience (Dewey 1934, p. 89).

Human subjects in *Leviathan* are all situated within an ecological and mechan-ical systemically intertwined realm of harshness and relentless toll on the physical body – all their dexterity is physical. *Leviathan* is about labor, but it is also about the coordinated destruction of natural resources through overfishing and disrupt-ing the bed of the ocean. It's about monumental scale, sweeping power and overnight, all-night plunder of the sea. The compositions of *Leviathan* are edited to maximize its impressionistic and painterly features. This approach submerges audiences into impressionistic vistas of weathered faces, orange smocks, netted gear, and decimated fish inside a claustrophobic world of visual and acoustic darkness. Fish heads and staring fish eyes and fish gore evoke the Spanish painter of war, persecution, and human agony, Goya.

Anyone who has been aboard a fishing vessel understands that day and night exist, yet Castaing-Taylor and Paravel chose to foreground darkness and the raw ecosystem as an experience. A fisherman falls asleep in a debris-strewn kitchen watching trash TV, exhausted. Is he finished with his shift, or merely taking a break? We will never know. Cigarettes hang out of fishermen's lips, indicating that their work takes a toll on their bodies in more than one way: extreme fatigue, the stimulant of nicotine, repetitive movements.

CASTAING-TAYLOR: This film is definitely invested in capturing realism. It's not acted, scripted or preordained in any way. It's a work of non-fiction, but it also feels fictional because it was created in the middle of this black, oceanic nowhere. It's a microcosm of the universe, which has no space-time bearings. It comes into being as its own progressive space, which seems fictional. I guess it's true that we see documentaries and most of them tend to bore us and we wouldn't want to make films that resemble them, especially because they aren't experimental and they're more concerned about telling you about the world and edify you or communicate something that is propagandistic ... We were interested in capturing this immediate and corporeal subjectiveness; a portrait of fishing from the inside where the cameras will capture the physicality of what it's like to be a fisherman ... we weren't so invested in the dialogue because it seems like such an incredibly thin, attenuative representation of the magnitude of human existence and the world itself. We decided to embrace the harsh sounds aboard the ship like the roaring engine, the sea, the labor on deck, the machines, the cables – they're all a part of the acoustic ecosystem.[19]

Conclusion

Sweetgrass and *Leviathan* are two strong examples of how video ethnography can evoke atmospheres or ambiences through experiential editing and experiential sounds in ways not possible in representational forms of research. Vannini (2014a, pp. 391–416) describes atmosphere as "ungraspable, indefinable, and only perceivable as fleeting moods, diffuse feelings and evanescent sensations." Video ethnography can provide an interpretive space through which audiences are able to reflect on relationships between humans and animals, and humans and machines, or humans and nature, to draw their own meaning and understanding of any given environment.

A key strength of video ethnography is how its methodological and editing choices – such as the selection of shots in close proximity to the object filmed – deliberately dislocate and estrange audiences. As demonstrated in *Sweetgrass* and

Leviathan, seeking ambiguity rather than clarity invites audiences to ask questions and figure out what's happening; to be active. However, as demonstrated, these choices also run the risk of boring and frustrating audiences. Regardless of the outcome, allowing audiences to focus on the sounds of raw atmosphere without signposting or contextualization emphasizes the experience of experiencing or the experiential. The darkness, for example, in *Leviathan* allows audiences to direct and attune their embodied senses to the sounds of the harsh atmosphere – so that audiences attune to the film physically through sense deprivation. As MacDougall (2006) points out, before a documentary is coherent, it is an arrangement of material properties including sounds, physical presences, gestures, and traces of encounters seen and heard through the filmmaker's camera, sound recorder, and ethnographic presence.

> We are in a different experiential world – one not necessarily inferior to reading a text, but to be understood differently. I believe we should not shy away from this pre-linguistic aspect of film and video … On the contrary, it allows us to reenter the corporeal spaces of our own and others' lives – the manner in which we all, as social creatures, assimilate forms and textures through our senses, learn things before we understand them, share experiences with others, and move through the varied social environments that surround us.
>
> *MacDougall 2006, p. 270*

The deliberately obfuscating approach to editing that I have described in this chapter, an approach that deliberately creates ambiguity, has enabled video ethnography to set new goals for researchers, allowing them to harness the ability to unsettle, estrange, and rework social realities (MacDougall 2006, p. 6). By going beyond the aim of merely attempting to represent an environment, or tell a story about it, video ethnography makes it possible to engage in the evoked real world in a more raw way; bringing with it the potential to transform understandings of everyday practices by bringing bodies, sounds, images, and worlds into new material relationship through film (MacDougall 2006, p. 7 same). By editing to emphasize the experiential, video ethnography invites audiences into expansive real worlds using editing to honor and accentuate the aesthetic of lived experience, its everyday textures, inherent drama, tensions, conflicts, and suspense – without creating story arcs or imposing narratives. As a medium of sensory expressivity and affective vitality, video ethnography shifts from representational textual evocation to a craft-orientated highly skilled and deliberate evocation of experiential flux. By implementing audiovisual technologies to interpretively record, edit, and evoke sensory properties, video ethnography amplifies lived experiences and exposes audiences to fluid, sonic, and expressive aspects of experience that could never be fully transmitted through post hoc textual description, or sometimes without the presence of verbal language at all as demonstrated in the next chapter.

Notes

1   https://unspokencinema.blogspot.com/2012/10/leviathan-paravelcastaing-taylor.html.
2   http://cinema-scope.com/cinema-scope-magazine/1107/.
3   http://cinema-scope.com/cinema-scope-magazine/1107/.
4   www.theartsdesk.com/film/director-lucien-castaing-taylor-making-sweetgrass.
5   http://pov-tc.pbs.org/pov/downloads/2011/pov-sweetgrass-discussion-guide-color.pdf.
6   https://filmmakermagazine.com/1402-lucien-castaing-taylor-ilisa-barbash-sweetgrass/.
7   www.inreviewonline.com/inreview/current_film/Entries/2010/3/1_Sweetgrass_%
    282010%29_Directed_by_Ilisa_Barbash_and_Lucien_Castaing-Taylor.htm.l
8   http://cinema-scope.com/cinema-scope-magazine/1107/.
9   http://cinema-scope.com/cinema-scope-magazine/1107/.
10 http://cinema-scope.com/cinema-scope-magazine/1107/.
11 http://cinema-scope.com/cinema-scope-magazine/1107/.
12 http://cinema-scope.com/cinema-scope-magazine/1107/.
13 www.theartsdesk.com/film/director-lucien-castaing-taylor-making-sweetgrass.
14 http://ohcomely.co.uk/ohcomely/2012/10/18/an-interview-with-directors-lucien-
    castaing-taylor-and-paravel.
15 https://unspokencinema.blogspot.com/2012/10/leviathan-paravelcastaing-taylor.html.
16 http://ohcomely.co.uk/stories/2012/10/18/an-interview-with-directors-lucien-castaing-
    taylor-and-paravel.
17 www.undertheradarmag.com/interviews/leviathans_directors_lucian_castaing-taylor
    _and_verena_paravel/.
18 www.undertheradarmag.com/interviews/leviathans_directors_lucian_castaing-taylor_and_
    verena_paravel/.
19 http://anthemmagazine.com/qa-with-lucien-castaing-taylor-verena-paravel/.

4

VIDEO ETHNOGRAPHY

Sanctuary as a case study

I have thus far argued that video ethnography is a burgeoning, open-ended methodological technique that crafts and evokes a distinct type of sensuous knowledge embedded in and arising from philosophical lineage of Merleau-Ponty's expressive phenomenology and Dewey's experiential pragmatism. This chapter examines my own documentary film, co-directed with my filmmaking partner Ashley Sabin, *Sanctuary*, as a case study that demonstrates how video ethnography draws upon expressive phenomenology and experiential pragmatism to explore donkeys' lived, corporeal experiences from within a donkey sanctuary. In this chapter I will chart how video ethnography is capable of crafting and evoking the lived experience of "donkey rehabilitation" as a form of sensuous scholarship.[1] *Sanctuary* deliberately emphasizes the distinct video ethnography methodologies described in this book to advance ethnographic media as a mode of sensory scholarship. I believe that, in order to challenge and overcome the domination of textual methodology, researchers must develop new visual and audio languages and sensibilities as described in previous chapters and forthcoming in this one. An academic project – such as video ethnography – that attempts to re-imagine and reconfigure audiovisual research should be, I believe, epistemologically and methodologically open-ended and emergent, subject to change, adaptation, and transformation. Lived experience cannot be directed or predicted prior to one's immersion in it, and the very act of recording lived experience is an act of altering and co-experiencing it. Again, to reiterate ideas discussed in Chapter 2, we cannot separate ourselves from lived sensuous experience; we are enmeshed in it and therefore *co-produce and co-create* it by inhabiting it. Methodologies that do not attune fully to the complex flux of lived experience are inadequate.

Where traditional representations of knowledge embrace *writing, arguing,* and *telling* as ways of knowing, video ethnography allows for far greater complexity through *showing, sensing, listening,* and *hearing* – and in so doing, helps us *relate* to experiences, especially those that are bodily, such as harm and rehabilitation (a prevalent theme of the film *Sanctuary*). Haptic and sensory experience of harm and rehabilitation evoked through video ethnographies has the power to emotively touch audiences, inspiring understanding and empathy.

Rather than dismissing video ethnography as an illegitimate video method that fails to conform to staple-of-the-discipline approaches to exploring lived experience, researchers might choose instead to expand their methodological sensibilities and to seek to extend and enhance understanding of sensuous knowledge production. As academics, we are taught – and we teach students – to write, read, and deliver textual research: we produce PowerPoints, Word documents, journal chapters, and books. Yet, in so doing, we reduce the plentitude of lived experience, in all its complexity and sensuousness, to written language and data – we hold ourselves back from plunging into the brute experiences of sound, smell, taste, perception, and color. In so doing we also reduce the possibility of empathy.

Today, opportunities exist that allow video ethnographers to go beyond the static methods of positivism, rational choice, and quantitative and qualitative research to explore mobile methods that can evoke and depict the fleeting, sensuous, and embodied motions of daily life. Les Back (2013) illustrates how today's academic environment increasingly encourages a broad imagination within the social sciences. "The tools and devices for research craft are being extended by digital culture in a hyper-connected world, affording new possibilities to re-imagine observation and the generation of alternative forms of research data" (Back and Puwar 2013, p. 7). The experiential flux of what people, objects, and animals (nonhuman humans) do can be depicted extensively and sensuously. Mobile methods of immersion can reside within the ambiguity of fluid and flux experiences. The methodological techniques of video ethnography allow researchers to depict lived experience in ways that written text cannot deliver.

Whereas written knowledge primarily lends itself to linear processing, sensory knowledge engages the viewer through nonlinear encounters and indeterminate contacts (MacDougall 2006). The video techniques of video ethnography conjoin sensory experience with corporeality to produce vibrant encounters. These techniques craft a sensory document that plunges viewers directly into fluctuating, lived experience by engaging pre-reflective, prelinguistic attention and through bodily expression. In the depiction of animals this is especially striking.

Sanctuary: context and frameworks

In journalistic realms and in the media in general, for example *The Economist,* the BBC, *The New York Times,* and *Nature,* the 21st century has been described as the *Anthropocene* – the "age of the human" – a new epoch defined by human devastation of the wild, natural world through acts of violence, domestication, and destruction. *Sanctuary* explores the broad ramifications of this epoch through the microcosm of animal rescue work, where the damage of human violence and cruelty against one particular species – the donkey – is addressed. Although the goal of donkey care work is to rehabilitate the health of damaged donkeys, the invasive animal husbandry measures required to achieve this goal inevitably inflict pain and fear in the greater interest of long-term improvement – even as they work to alleviate the ravages of human cruelty. The invasive procedures necessary to rescue donkeys from cruelty render them dependent on their human caretakers. Donkeys cannot decide when, where, or what to eat; they are not free to leave; they are bound by the institution's spatial and temporal barriers, put in place to protect and heal them. Within this mandatory enclosure, many of the donkeys are cut off from the wider ecology forever, sutured between a cruel world of deliberate abuse and the inadvertent but inevitable pain of rehabilitation. A central ethnographic question explored in *Sanctuary* through cinematic means is: how do donkeys inhabit, embody, and expressively experience this institutional space of care work that initially subjects them to distress in order to deliver a life of safety and security against cruelty and neglect?

Most audiences expect, from any film, a narrative arc, or, in other words, a beginning, middle, and end with plot, tension, protagonist, and antagonist. The approach to narrative in *Sanctuary* avoids this standard trajectory, foregoing "plot" resolution in favor of prioritizing tactile experiences that are also ambiguous or left unexplained. These surplus-seeming experiences are often eliminated from stories that use exposition and interviews to signpost and frame the film's sensory material in the interests of clarity, achieved through language. In *Sanctuary* they are included: for example, the messy, unpleasant, and, at times, alarming moments of animal husbandry – a needle in a donkey's neck, surgery to repair wounds and legacies of neglect, farriers slicing into donkey hooves. *Sanctuary* unsettles audiences at a visceral level and troubles the conscience, while also instilling in audiences the vital sensory experiences that allow them to affectively attune to the vulnerability of others – in this case, bestial others.

Sanctuary attempts to plunge viewers directly into the fluid nonverbal experiences of donkeys through their pre-reflective attention and external expressivity inside a contained environment that Goffman refers to as a "total institution." Goffman (1961, p. 11) defines a total institution as "a place of residence and work where a large number of like-situated individuals, cut off from the wider society for an appreciable period of time, together lead an enclosed, formally administered round of life." As a video ethnographer, my wider objective is to make a significant methodological contribution to audiovisual sentient research. My aim is to craft an ethnographic documentary that immerses audiences into how donkeys expressively reside in a human-made total institution. These empirical depictions entail showing and hearing the patterns of donkeys' everyday experiences – their movements, sounds (e.g., brays, communication), ways of walking, eating, using space, and how they perceive their environment.

Donkey representation

Donkeys are "actors" in several movies and documentaries, although are rarely at the center of any story. Buñuel's *Land without Bread* opens with a donkey walking on a street closely followed by a horse. Thirteen minutes later a donkey is shown attacked by bees while tied to a log. Apparently, Buñuel poured honey on the donkey's skin so he could film bees attacking the animal. A few seconds later the same donkey is dead with a patchwork of bees swarming across its face. Buñuel and his team of filmmakers inflicted torture and killed a donkey to obtain a 30-second shot.

Sweetgrass shows a string of mules carrying a load of supplies for sheepherders and cowboys against the backdrop of mountains. Robert Bresson's revered *Au hasard Balthazar* is an exception in how it pushes cinematographic boundaries in its depiction of the relationship between the abused donkey, Balthazar, and its (often cruel) human caretakers. Whereas *Au hasard Balthazar* chronicles the longitudinal experiences of a single donkey over its lifetime, *Sanctuary* examines the broader conditions of harm and healing encountered by donkeys residing inside care work institutions. Countless other movies contain background images of donkeys passing through and across landscapes. *Sanctuary*'s camera and sound methodologies, by contrast, foreground donkeys and their brays, trots, and ways of negotiating space as they move through a total institution. *Sanctuary* shows experiential images and sounds that observe how donkeys' lives are shaped, orchestrated, and managed inside the sanctuary's total institution.

A central methodological tenet of video ethnography is learning to attend to the activity within which the research/filmmaker is engaged by placing one's body close to it. This proximate relationship enables continuous attention to the subject. It requires adjusting the positioning of the camera to the movements all around. In *Sanctuary* the donkeys' movements (feet shuffling, ears flapping, heads bowed eating) and their brays give the film the look and feel of a choreographed piece. All of these moments are mundane, but when given fuller attention they create a symphony of movement, sound, and emotion. How the audience is transported into the donkey's daily rhythms and patterns depends on where the camera is placed (and for how long) in relation to the donkey's spatial awareness, pace, and movement. This experiential approach absorbs viewers in the minutiae and range of donkey life with long-take shots.

Sanctuary experiments with long, unbroken shots designed to evoke the continuity of lived experience. The drama of duration produces shots that are mundane yet highly charged, attuned to everyday moments of texture and sound. Without the aid of voice-over or expert interviews, the audience is left to engage directly with donkeys in a sensory way. Slow movements and extended duration offer audiences the opportunity to thoughtfully reflect on their relationship with the animals, and with their nonlinguistic yet expressive, atmospheric soundscape. *Sanctuary* opens up a rare moment for viewers, allowing them to be actively present in the life of another species as the animals experience their expressive world, without the narration or signposting of, say, a nature documentary.

Sanctuary arrives during a particularly crucial period for animal rights, as capitalism fuels the growth of urbanization and consumerism encourages expansive development without regard for the impact on other species that share our planet. Today, fewer and fewer "wild" spaces remain in which donkeys and other animals can live without human intervention. According to the World Wildlife Fund, the planet has seen a 50% reduction in the overall number of wild animals since 1975[2]; carbon emissions, urban expansion, pollution, abuse, and trafficking are pushing the wilderness to the margins. Into the breach created by this global crisis, institutions have arisen to protect marginalized animals and the environments they inhabit. *Sanctuary* focuses on the rehabilitation of one particular species as an analog for the larger issues of animal rights and ecojustice.

Once highly valued as agricultural and transportation tools, donkeys in the postindustrial world have been rendered superfluous. As their functional value in society has diminished, so hundreds of thousands of donkeys have been re-commodified. There are increasingly criminal networks that illegally traffic donkeys, selling them to factory farms where they are slaughtered, processed, and falsely packaged as "beef" in France, Sweden, Canada, South Africa, Australia, the USA, the UK, and other countries. State complicity in the abusive treatment of animals is rampant: the Parks and Wildlife Department and the Bureau of Land Management in the United States routinely round up and shoot donkeys; in Mexico, China, and in Canada, donkey hides are sold and carcasses are butchered as meat; Taliban and ISIS fighters sometimes plant bombs in donkeys, and military soldiers kill donkeys suspected of transporting armed weapons for terrorists.

To date, over 100,000 donkeys have been rescued from abuse and abandonment in the UK, the USA, France, Spain, Canada, and Ireland. This startling number of rescues raises crucial questions: why are so many donkeys abandoned and abused in so-called developed countries? What does this behavior imply about humankind's relationship to these "useless" or redundant creatures whose labour once crucially facilitated the development of civilization? Today, more than 50 million donkeys continue to guarantee subsistence for people in low-income parts of the world who rely on them as transport and farm animals.

In response to the ongoing decimation of wild animals in the Anthropocene epoch, a burgeoning "rewilding" movement in contemporary culture is reintroducing formerly wild species into their original ecological niches. Academic conferences have been convened to consider the complicated relationships between the Anthropocene, the wild, humans, and animals. Movies, documentaries, and fiction films featuring animals are on the rise (e.g., *Blackfish, Sweetgrass, Kedi, Racing Extinction, Virunga*), heralding the birth of a new domain in film studies called "Ecocinema" which explores possibilities for coexistence among animals, the ecology, and humankind. Netflix, National Geographic, and the Discovery Channel are all currently developing programs on wildlife, animals, and the last remaining "wild" spaces on earth (e.g., NAT GEO WILD).

Video ethnography as sensuous scholarship

Video ethnography's wider objective is invitational. Uninterested in grand theory, it embraces a perspective-orientated approach that seeks to develop methodologically open-ended and porous sensibilities that are permitted to evolve and adapt over time. Unlike textual scholarship, which relies primarily on written language for analysis, video ethnography crafts an aesthetically rich, empirical, sensuous scholarship that uses images, sounds, and textures to immerse audiences in evocative lived experience. Video ethnography attends to lyrical impressions and atmospheres of lived experience. To paraphrase Jane Bennett (2009), video ethnography's sensuous knowledge is *vibrant*; it provides an experiential way of knowing and transfigures the real through contact and encounter. When we engage with video ethnography, we not only know the real intellectually: we also *encounter* the real with our bodies prelinguistically as indicated by Marks (2000) in Chapter 1. We are sensual and bodily before we are verbal; we are pre-reflective and reflective creatures. Video ethnography's phenomenological framework "calls us to a series of systematic reflections within which we question and clarify that which we intimately live, but which has been lost to our reflective knowledge through habituation and/or institutionalization" (Sobchack 1992, p. 28). The unique window video ethnography provides into lived experience broadens a researcher's boundaries.

Video ethnography and the age of the "Anthropocene"

Academics have published poignant and divergent literature on the *Anthropocene* – the "age of the human" – a questionable new epoch defined by human devastation of ecological habitat through acts of destruction (Baskin 2015; Bonneuil and Fressoz 2015; Hamilton et al. 2015; Pattberg and Zelli 2016; Ruddiman 2003; Steffen et al. 2011). An Anthropocene framework pursues an exploration of how media represents harm against species, ecology, and humankind. For example, Kohm and Greenhill (2013, p. 376) observe that media's "affective nuances" can engage audiences and "open up spaces for affective engagement with (in)justice and simultaneously suggests a re-examination of taken-for-granted assumptions about offending and harm and their connection to broader contexts." Indeed, such quintessentially mainstream companies as Netflix, National Geographic, CNN, BBC, ARTE, Amazon, and the Discovery Channel are currently developing and expanding programs on the problematic relationships between animals and humans. The majority of these "wild" documentaries appear in public platforms such as iTunes, TV stations, open-access e-journals with video embeds, film festivals, galleries, and movie theaters.

"Wild" as a concept that is inseparable from nature and culture – and especially media depictions of both – has been a debate among academics. Cronon's (1995) argument, for instance, is that "wild" is fundamentally a human creation seeped in value-laden Romanticism that elevates it to the status of the sacred and divorces humans from the natural. Drawing upon the discourse of poets and environmental activists, Cronon demonstrates the human construction of wild as supernatural, transcendental, classist, and often racist. Yet, according to Cronon, "wild" is everywhere; it contains its own autonomy and reasons for being inside ecological relationships increasingly becoming decimated, protected, and documented by media (Cronon 1995). Media's entangled relationship with the wild is contradictory, as will be explored in the concluding critiques of this chapter.

Methodological sensibilities: four approaches to evoking aspects of the Anthropocene

Sanctuary took three months to prepare and five years to make. In our filmmaking, my partner Ashley Sabin and I acted initially as trained ethnographers. We relied on the attuned skills of patience, participation, and immersive participatory-observation while taking detailed notes. We remained stationary in various parts of the sanctuary for several days – at times, we slept there for up to seven nights; when not overnighting at the sanctuary, we slept in an adjacent bungalow for up to a month at a time, off and on for five years. Our goal in undergoing this immersion was to understand the rhythms and sounds of rehabilitation, the everyday quotidian movements through which humans and donkeys encounter each other during care work procedures, and the haptic interactions of touch as a rehabilitative process. We gave particular attention to the rhythms and patterns of caretakers and their choreographic gestures, how they delivered and isolated the donkeys to provide rehabilitation from abuse. We incorporated our observations into the techniques we used to move and place our camera and sound recorder in relation to the rehabilitation process.

From our initial immersive activities, we decided to focus on and implement four methodological techniques: (1) learning to attend, (2) using the continuous long-take, (3) sensory reliance, and (4) sonic communication. I believe each of these techniques are central to video ethnography as described in Chapter 1. In the next pages, I will use *Sanctuary* as a case study to explore ways in which to extend video ethnography into a practice-based methodology of audiovisual sensory scholarship that crafts evocative, immersive media out of lived experiences. The four methodological techniques of video ethnography identified contribute to the production of new evocative sensuous scholarship. I will now describe how adding to these four methods, researchers can advance understanding even more deeply.

The techniques I will outline are crucial for evoking first, an "order of things," (Bennett 2009), second, the structure of an experience (Sniadecki 2014), and last, atmospheric drama in the mundane experiences of situational care work (Vannini 2015a). In the following pages I will relate some of the aspects of video ethnology previously discussed in this book in preceding pages to these three new notions. For example, *learning to attend* and the *continuous long-take* are crucial methodologies for facilitating *sensory reliance* which "proceeds neither through the reductionism of abstract language nor the subordination of image and sound to argument, but instead through the expansive potential of aesthetic experience and experiential knowledge" (Sniadecki 2014, p. 26). Finally, *sonic communication* which allows viewers to appreciate that meaning "does not emerge only from language; it engages with the ways in which our sensory experience is pre- or nonlinguistic, and part of our bodily being in the world."[3] In the rest of this chapter, I will discuss how these four methodologies are used to enhance and deepen the empathic experience of *Sanctuary*.

1 Learning to attend: rehabilitation through touch

If learning to attend forms a central tenet of video ethnography then in *Sanctuary*, attending to and foregrounding the role of touch is a crucial aspect of evoking donkey rehabilitative experience, since touch is the first form of interaction or experience used in rehabilitating abused and abandoned donkeys. In *Sanctuary*, the minutia of donkey care work accentuates the role of touch and the haptic. Human hands move across the body of an abused donkey; a woman calmly speaks to donkeys while stroking them. Long duration shots amplify this emphasis on touch. As referenced in Chapter 1 of this book, Marks writes suggestively about touch and haptic criticism to discuss mimetic representation (Marks 2000, p. xii). "Haptic criticism is mimetic: it presses up to the object and takes its shape. Mimesis is a form of representation based on getting close enough to the other thing to become it" (Marks 2000, p. xiii). Also mimetic are the sounds of *Sanctuary* which are recorded and edited to be loud and haptic so that a donkey braying may cause a haptic stirring in the chest that allows audiences to experience the donkey's presence, and even the emotional register of the braying, within their bodies.

As filmmakers creating this kind of haptic or mimetic video ethnography, based in proximity, training oneself to attend closely to haptic means attuning closely to subjects and their environment, thereby co-constructing involvement as a *relationship*. Close together in space, collaborative dynamics emerge between the video ethnographer, the donkeys, and their human caretakers, concentrating around moments of care-giving. These shared dynamics converge to produce what Manning and Massumi (2014, p. 92) call a "catalyzing moment" that helps the situation develop a "creative participation which would be encouraged to take on their shape, direction, and momentum in the course of the event" (Manning and Massumi 2014, p. 92).

Manning and Massumi (2014) refer to the methodological approach of learning to attend as "techniques of relation." According to their formulation, techniques of relation always occur within "enabling constraints" and are therefore devices for catalyzing and modulating interaction; they comprise of a domain of *practices* (Manning and Massumi 2014, p. 91). In the making of *Sanctuary* we, the filmmakers, by attending closely to donkeys and their caretakers during acts of caretaking explore these relational moments in open-ended ways through our camera and sound recorder. "This means that what is key is less what ends are pre-envisioned – or any kind of subjective intentional structure – than how the initial conditions for unfolding are set" (Manning and Massumi 2014, p. 89).

Learning to attend is a skilled practice that brings all sensing and decision-making faculties of the filmmaker into play as an intuitive form of mobile flexibility that can be described as "wild," meaning spontaneous and deft. This kind of attuned wildness allows the filmmaker to attend quickly to unforeseen possibilities, unexpected practices, and new types of movements as they unfold. As discussed earlier in this book in relation to SEL's open-ended approach to filmmaking, video ethnography films tend not to be planned in advance or carried out to support a preconceived idea of vision, but take their own shape, form, and momentum to arrive at an unknown outcome.

2 Long-take: duration of an experience

As discussed, long shots help accentuate raw and strange sounds like braying and experiences of touch, making *Sanctuary* an extremely haptic experience as a film. *Sanctuary* deliberately uses long, unbroken shots in order to more fully explore the expressivity of the donkey experience of rehabilitation within the sanctuary habitat. Slow movements and extended scenes offer audiences the opportunity to bodily adjust to the donkeys' pace, the spaces in which rehabilitation occurs, and the nonlinguistic soundscapes of the world of donkey rehabilitation. The use of long-takes in *Sanctuary* invites viewers into the more subtle aspects of rehabilitating donkeys without the kind of explanations and signposting of, for example, a veterinary or animal rescue TV show, allowing them to observe and draw their own conclusions or make inferences about the donkeys' experience of being both contained and cared for, in a newly assembled herd. *Sanctuary* opens up a rare moment in the lives of viewers, allowing them to be actively present during the rehabilitation of donkeys and exposing them to the tension inherent in this process.

The film's long-take shots wordlessly explore how donkeys progress from newly rescued to settled within the sanctuary, from arrival to isolation, grooming (clipping, bathing, dangerously overgrown and neglected hooves pared) to their introduction to the rest of the herd and eventual membership of the herd. As video ethnographers we seek to give audiences the space and time through long-take shots to sensuously understand the length of time it takes to heal invisible and visible wounds. Experiential long-takes provide audiences an opportunity to connect (or to "cathect") with donkeys during the rehabilitative process, and to imagine what each animal might be feeling and experiencing (guesswork that is actively imaginative, connecting with the "otherness" of a domesticated wild animal).

Cathexis is "the process of charging an object, activity, or place with emotional energy, which is in turn related to memory creation" (Pretty 2013, p. 493). Video ethnography's advantage in this case is its ability to evoke highly charged situations and to appeal to the affective nature of the senses, rather than to a cerebral or information-based response. Brisman and South (2014, p. 57) suggest that cathexis facilitates "attachment to objects, activities, and places, and this matures over time as a part, and as a reflection, of biography and experience." While Brisman and South use the term "cathexis" to critically consider the limitations of consumerism, their use of the term can be applied to empathic and sensuous interaction between viewers and abused donkeys, catalyzed during highly charged circumstances. Cathexis suggests that viewers may construct an attachment to animals, so that eventually the affective charge becomes part of their own autobiographical identity. Video ethnography is inherently an experiential and sensuous medium and, for this reason, the technique of the long-take has the potential to connect, or cathect, donkeys with viewers.

The long-take intentionally eschews expository narrative and avoids constructing tension through the juxtaposition of shots in cinema verité style or with the use of words. Instead, the long-take closely resembles Scott MacDonald's (2013) phenomenological pragmatism: it evokes brute lived experience shaped into a narrative of everyday encounters, where the tension resides *within* the shot rather than *between* the juxtapose shots. The long-takes presented in *Sanctuary* shift the presentation of lived experience away from a dramatic, edited narrative, to an attuned phenomenological inquiry of presence. Therefore any overt or explicit narrative of "animal rescue" is omitted, while instead a defamiliarized and haptic, nonnarrative approach unfolds.

Long-takes also serve to elucidate the structure of an experience and reveal drama in everyday, seemingly ordinary or mundane situational moments. The long-take allows us as filmmakers to attend closely to the open-ended intersections and junctions of human and animal interaction in the name of rehabilitation. As filmmakers and as viewers, understanding rehabilitation entails paying close attention to animal body language and ambiance: how donkeys position themselves to eat, where they stand, and how they move in synchronistical rhythms toward and within barriers of spatial limitations and freedoms. The camera is positioned to gaze upon donkeys held captive within walls, yet donkeys look back at the camera with their own inscrutable or only partially apparent emotions and intentions, building in a reflexive moment to our filmmaking. Their gaze holds the audience, with the plentitude of their animal selves and their mystery. It is clear that donkeys are not only objects to be looked at; as in the sheep in *Sweetgrass*, they are subjects who stare back.

3 Sensory reliance

The mechanical sounds of a horse trailer clanking mingle with a donkey's muffled snorts. Where is the donkey going and why? Nothing is explicitly explained; instead audiences rely on their senses through an introductory long-take shot as *Sanctuary* follows a donkey entering an institution, a presumed sanctuary. As an audience we see that there are more donkeys than this new arrival – thousands more. Dwelling largely on the activities of this herd, the film unfolds as a curiosity-provoking exploration, through sounds and gestures, without words, or titles, or voice-over. Without the aid of voice-over or expert interviews, the audience is left to sensuously engage directly with a world of sensory textures and kinetic inflections. This is pure video ethnography, a cinematic aesthetic that strives to use crafted media to situate audiences inside immersive phenomena with a feeling of deep personal presence rather than to explain or signpost using text or words.

When words, titles, and the human language are stripped away from documentary films and when viewers must rely on their own interpretive skills to experience the documentary *the documentary itself is the analysis*. Video ethnography's methodological technique of "sensory reliance" is open-ended, freeing, and expansive. It allows audiences to collaboratively interpret films through their own sensory engagement and imagination; as an approach, it fosters instincts such as attentiveness and patience, like a wild environment that requires a natural historian's approach to sensing and observing rather than knowing. The role of the senses and of haptic experience is elevated.

Instead of subordinating lived experiences as topics for linguistic or expert explanation, *Sanctuary* reaches beyond verbal, numerical, and textual research and forms of knowledge to embrace sensory scholarship, raw, unfolding lived experience, and tactile or haptic sensations transmitted to the viewer's body through movement, sound, and visual texture. Engaging audiences' senses the film immerses audiences in the donkeys' institutional habitat and in rehabilitative scenes that are open-ended "as seen, felt, and heard – they speak to the body ..." (Redmon 2015, p. 435). The idea of animal abuse, neglect, and harm in *Sanctuary* is offered as a puzzle to be teased out (Brisman and South 2013, p. 125).

In *Sanctuary*, audiences experience repeated scenes involving touch, so prevalent in the world of donkey rehabilitation depicted, as they simultaneously feel touched by the visceral, sensorial presentation of this world. John Dewey (1934, p. 224) quotes a poet who maintains that

> poetry seemed "more physical than intellectual," and goes on to say that he recognizes poetry by physical symptoms such as bristling of the skin, shivers in the spine, constriction of the throat, and a feeling in the pit of the stomach like Keats' "spear going through me."

This physical, sensory, poetic mode is true of *Sanctuary* as a cinematic experience: the eeriness of the dark barn, the closeness of donkey fur, the varied loud sounds of the distinctive donkey bray, and direct sensory interconnection felt through the donkey's gaze – all generate tension felt by and within the body. These aural and tactile experiences are haptic, intended to activate audiences' bodies, senses, and minds – thereby providing a "thick" understanding of what abused donkeys go through during the process of rehabilitation.

Sanctuary is an example of how video ethnography tends to approach the human/nonhuman barrier as a realm of negative capability – an opportunity to explore relational sentience across species difference. A larger objective of video ethnography is to sensuously inflect and infuse these human/nonhuman differences with vitality so they flourish and expand rather than diminish. Video ethnography helps to promote expansive thinking about animals and interspecies relationships. By immersing audiences in sounds and visuals that foster haptic contact, video ethnographers are able to open up audiences to new ways of seeing, sensing, and becoming aware of animals' lives and interspecies relationships without passively relying on traditional forms of "expertise" or commentary. *Sanctuary* allows audiences to forge new relationships with an animal species in crisis and stirs empathy in ways that depart from traditional use of tropes of sentiment, pity, anthropomorphism, or heroism.

4 Sonic communication and diegetic sound

Sonic communication and diegetic sound, meaning sounds naturally occurring or arising from what we see, have an affect on our bodies, especially when the sound is striking or unusual. *Sanctuary* maximizes the impact of diegetic donkey and ambient sounds, and minimizes spoken human language. Approximately seven English sentences are spoken in *Sanctuary*; overwhelmingly, the soundscape is mechanical, animal, and environmental.

Banging metal bars clash with donkey brays; the sounds of impatient donkeys thudding in a soft-floored barn comingle with the echoes and refractions of their hooves trotting across the concrete floors as they face getting dosed with medicine. The sounds of donkeys jumping, resisting their medicine, and licking their lips blend with donkey brays in the background. These atmospheric sounds of the flux of donkey rehabilitation communicate phenomenological experience. In films about animals or nature documentaries, it seems we are so acclimated to the presence of an expository, disembodied voice directing viewers' attention that the mere omission of this voice starkly foregrounds the ambiguity of sonic language. This style makes *Sanctuary* feel radically wild, vibrant, and open-ended.

Sanctuary reflects video ethnography's methodological advantage of fostering immediate sensory immersion in the experience depicted, as a form of aesthetic knowledge. Video ethnographies of this kind are also able to use sensuous scholarship to communicate sonic textures from multiple perspectives, bringing a sense of beyond human sensory experience into the mix. For example, in *Sanctuary* audiences learn about all the material aspects of donkey rehabilitation, and damage, and neglect repair through sound: the sound of repairing donkey teeth; the grating of filing down overgrown, neglected donkey hooves; the tactile softness of massaging a sore. These sensory encounters activate viewers' bodies in uncomfortable and engaged ways. The sound of the donkey dentist's machine grinding on the enamel of donkey teeth is a crucial part of rehabilitation and forms a routine part of the donkey sanctuary's sonic environment. These sounds agitate and vibrate, evoking memories in viewers of their own experiences of being treated at the dentist, or treating their own animals, and stirs identification and empathy. The oblique, nonnarrative style of *Sanctuary* means that the world of donkey rehabilitation is apprehended in sensuous, sonic ways. The need for rehabilitation arising from abuse and neglect that would ordinarily be more explicitly signposted in a conventional animal rescue or vérité documentary goes unmentioned, yet is subtly implied. In this way audiences listen to the "rough music" of the consequences of donkey harm and neglect through routine care work, as the film's underlying theme of harm appears to lie beyond, fostering curiosity, but prioritizing the bodily and our own sensory connection to the animal before any cerebral, ethical, or judgmental set of categories, ideas that go unmentioned.

The visceral sounds of rehabilitation communicate nonverbally through aesthetic experience, and in the unsaid the reality of the harm done to these animals is even more present, because it is so physical. These diegetic and depicted sounds of video ethnography communicate obliquely yet also in very direct ways, straight into the audiences' bodies, to replace and surpass what a textual or informational form of communication – a title or a voice-over – would ordinarily do. Experiencing the pain and necessity of medicalized veterinary rehabilitation becomes visceral, immediate, and shared. Video ethnography works on the premise that sound is felt internally and externally on the eardrum and reverberates throughout the skin of the body. In the words of Max Goldberg, a Museum of the Moving Image journalist, "Sound is channeled rather than framed: this basic fact is fundamental to SEL's underlying goal of anthropology by other means – in a word, embodiment."[4]

It is an important source of sensory and communicative information that is all too often overlooked. The soundscapes of video ethnography tend to immerse the body in an experience of the sonic that is largely an overlooked aspect of lived experience in research methods, a last methodological frontier. Researchers almost never study the sounds of lived aesthetic experience, and when they do they tend to write about them descriptively rather than use sound mimetically. Most conventional documentary films subjugate sound so that it plays a supporting role only to the visual. Video ethnography is a field in which sonic forms of aesthetic communication and information are treated with equal emphasis and care if not more attention and care than visual and textual representation. While the "visual" in "visual studies" is often privileged, video ethnography stands out for being as interested in the invisible as much as in the visible (Davies et al., 2014), and it is through its attention to the sonic realm that video ethnography seems to have an edge over other forms of research in its methodological and epistemological capacity for prioritizing the affective sonic channel of haptic experience.

In *Sanctuary*, it's precisely this attuned sonic approach that translates the film's oblique theme of the impact of abuse and neglect into an active, affective experience that provide audiences with a crucial interpretive key to understanding the world the film explores. Like *Leviathan* and *Sweetgrass*, *Sanctuary* demonstrates the power of sonic presence and soundscapes as forms of aesthetic knowledge that are treated with equal weight to visual streams. Like *Leviathan* and *Sweetgrass*, *Sanctuary* elevates the role of sound to surpass its usual role as a supplementary aspect of documentary film, used to aid visual and textual representation, or as a literal music soundtrack used to guide audience emotion.

Conclusion

My discussion of my documentary film *Sanctuary* offers the film as a case study that demonstrates four methodological techniques of video ethnography that contribute in powerful ways to the emerging field of sensory scholarship: (1) learning to attend, (2) using the continuous long-take, (3) sensory reliance, and (4) sonic communication. As discussed, *Sanctuary* deploys these techniques in order to engage audiences in sensuously appreciating the experience of rehabilitative process donkeys undergo when recovering from abuse and neglect.

The four techniques outlined in this chapter are in no way definitive or rule-based, and can be explored and adapted in open-ended ways that allow video ethnographers to craft sensory experience that is dynamic, engaged, and attuned to all forms of sensory experience emerging from direct encounters. These methodological techniques should be understood in a context of flexible expectations. Video ethnography takes place through actual practice and through ongoing encounters in the field. The researcher's approach is attuned to the rhythms, dynamics, and ambiguity of lived experience. The experiential nature of this approach sets video ethnography fundamentally apart from other, more textually-based research. It will also continue to evolve as technology itself evolves. Fundamentally, while not a rule, I believe that the sensory-based methodology of video ethnography, broadly speaking, sets out to explore: *how is it possible to understand and relate to lived experience in ways that help to raise questions about it?*

I couch this question deliberately in ways that are relational, tentative, and suggestive in order to posit an epistemological reconfiguration of the cinematic imagination and our methodological approaches as video ethnographers. *Sanctuary*, for example, seeks to relate lived experience, in its case nonhuman or animal, in ways that are sensory-based and that involve audience's bodies, through the senses, in the meaning of damage, abuse, neglect, and harm.

I have also borrowed extensively from ethnography's open-ended ideas about "wild" or brute methodologies, discussing how to bring experiential approaches into play in mobile encounters that allow researchers to move deftly with the flux of sensory experience. I have also addressed how video ethnography has been able to find a sizeable public nonspecialist audience, because its films are often appreciated for their bold aesthetics and atmosphere. I have discussed how video ethnography is able to create new forms of sensory scholarship that reimagines the relationship between public audiences and academic researchers by pointing out how many of video ethnography's key works are currently disseminated on a range of popular platforms, including iTunes, Netflix, Vudu, and in "theatrical release" through movie theaters (Vannini 2016).

Notes

1 *Sanctuary* can viewed at the following link: https://vimeo.com/176517219 with the password: greenculture.
2 www.theguardian.com/environment/2014/sep/29/earth-lost-50-wildlife-in-40-years-wwf.
3 https://earroom.wordpress.com/2013/02/14/ernst-karel/.
4 www.movingimagesource.us/articles/signal-to-noise-20130228.

5

GIRL MODEL

A case study in the methods and ethics of video ethnography[1]

In the previous chapter I examined editing choices in *Sanctuary* and related them as a significant contribution to the advancement of methodological techniques in the social sciences. This chapter examines methodological and ethical choices in my documentary *Girl Model* (codirected with Ashley Sabin) as an example of the additional shaping influence and legacies of ethnographic practices taught in academic departments. As the previous chapter discussed, academic departments have recently turned toward the sensory, sonic, and audiovisual tools as part of a burgeoning video methodology exploring aspects of sensuousness (Vannini 2017). This newly emerging emphasis on the sensuous has led academics to interact in many nuanced ways with documentary films: they appear in documentaries; they use documentaries in classes to illustrate concepts; they analyze and interpret documentaries in the context of their research. However, it seems that very few academics are able to find the infrastructural institutional support necessary to produce this kind of emergent sensuous knowledge in video ethnography or documentary film form. While the proliferation of audiovisual technology and media software, together with the turn toward investigating lived sensory experience, has helped develop a framework for video methodologies within academic disciplines – disciplines that have, for far too long, relied on words to communicate findings – I believe there is still too much talking and writing in academia and not enough sensuous evocation. While written observation and a lot of explaining and critiquing abound, there remains very little showing, sounding, and listening. Written analysis and discursive interpretation of media is a staple of the discipline, yet the use of audiovisual technology to *craft* sensory media is currently negligible.

Girl Model is framed by aspects of experiential cinema identified in previous chapters, but it is also a work of montage and character studies. The film draws upon the notion of supply chains in how it follows the circulation of teenage girls who are "discovered" by Russian and American scouts as Russian "models." The film initially started as an attempt to understand the motivations of one of the main characters, Ashley the model scout, but during the making of the project it became an exploration of the circulation of young girls who become part of an international industry of commodified labor. *Girl Model* draws upon the experiential cinema of David MacDougall in that it opens with a long-take of young girls in Novosibirsk, Russia who are auditioning as models, whereas other sections draw upon verbal interviews while people are doing activities and participating in the modeling endeavors. Overall, the aim of the film is to self-reflexively immerse viewers into the ethics of the situation by filming experiential situations as they unfold rather than directing the experiences. That is, the film explores what Grimshaw and Ravetz (2009, p. 81) refer to as the "concrete details and processes of material life." *Girl Model* does so by visually and aurally attending to experiential fabrics of the space and the sounds throughout the girls' journeys. Each character overlaps once or twice in the film, thereby illustrating how global ethnography and video ethnography simultaneously can cohabitate as a method and ethics of practice in an experiential manner. The film otherwise has no plot: it zigzags from France to the United States, from France to Japan, and other locations, delicately observing and reflexively listening and participating with each character.

Evoking these experiences and crafting them as fragments of moments certainly reduces the enormity of the situation to a palimpsest glimpse of the experiences of the people in the film – and the viewpoint of the filmmaker – but also shows the disorientations and alienation of the characters as they pursue, or get lost in, their efforts. *Girl Model* is a film that explores ethics while simultaneously constructing those ethics for the viewer to encounter on the skin of their body (Marks 2000). As indicated by Grimshaw and Ravetz, the problem here is how to avoid "aestheticizing one's subjects, or using subjects in the service of an artistic vision" (2009, p. 146). Therefore, *Girl Model* engages experiential situations while also inserting a self-reflexive methodology and ethics of participation between filmmaker and filmed. It does so in three ways: through responsive, interactive, and constructive techniques (MacDougall 2006). That is, by observing and interpreting

> its subject without provoking or disturbing [them]. It responds rather than interferes. An interactive camera, on the contrary, records its own interchanges with the subject. A constructive camera interprets its subject by breaking it down and reassembling it according to some external logic.
>
> *MacDougall 2006, p. 4*

MacDougall's analysis here doesn't explore a fourth option of his participatory ethnography explanation: an experiential approach to ethics and participant relationship. An experiential approach includes all three techniques while integrating them into a material fabric that "reflects the interplay between meaning and being, and its meaning takes into account the autonomy of being. Meaning can easily overpower being" (MacDougall 2006, p. 4). An experiential relationship considers the relations between humans, objects and nonhumans within the fabrics of *perceptive* existence – living and nonhuman (Merleau-Ponty 1965). Here, the ethics of the filmmaker – and those who are filmed – are woven into the textures of the film as a tactile experience that establishes close connections with the subjects and audiences through a methodological immersion that touches the viewer (Barker 2009). The audience, filmmaker, and subjects all share the experience: "texture, spatial orientation, comportment, rhythm, and vitality" (Barker 2009, p. 2). The ambiguity resides in the lack of clarity on how the filmmaker presents their own ethical stance because of the proximity of their body in relation to the subject being filmed – the filmmaker often avoids filming "close-ups" in favor of positioning his or her body "up close" with the experience – and then presenting this relationship *as an experience* to the viewer. Thus, viewers must interpret the situation in an open-ended, tacit, and implicit way without overt and explicit direction or instruction by the filmmaker.

Closeness is often equated with intimacy but it can have an opposite affect too: discomfort, ambiguity, and disorientation, especially when the filmic situation is ethically problematic. In this situation the filmmaker acknowledges and includes their own participation within the ethics of the film and the ethics of the situation – a point explored in more detail at the end of this chapter – to exude the tactile discomfort of the situation rather than hide, disguise, or avoid it. In other words, the filmmaker elects to include the experiential textures into the very fabric of the film in order to evoke the comfort and discomfort to the bodies of the viewers, thereby posing the following question cinematically: what would you do? Vannini (2015a, pp. 123–125) describes this approach as an immediacy of experience that is concerned with embodiment and emplacement, all of which resides within the theoretical precursors presented in Chapter 2.

> The immediacy of the ethnographer's experiences and their evocations are informed by temporalities, such as rhythmical recurrences (e.g., minutes, hours, days, weeks, seasons, years), the duration of events, the speed of various processes, the elusiveness and unpredictability of happenings, and the contested, contradictory, and conflicted practices through which virtual futures are actualized. In simpler words, a concern with the immediacy of ethnographic animation is a concern with its embodied and emplaced "live" nature – for example, the here and now of field experience – as much as with the intricacies of that present moment ... Emplaced ethnographies pay attention to how embodied experiences of the field are colored by the many properties – the sights, sounds, textures, smells, tastes, temperatures, movements – of place. These and other spatialities of the field must be tended to, reflected upon, cultivated, and carefully evoked ... Ethnographic representation, therefore, deeply relies on proximity.

Video ethnography evokes and fully embraces the proximity of experiences as closeness in a relational way: to the body, the perceiver, and the subject/filmmaker as ethical, methodological, and theoretical reflexivity. An experiential approach to ethics comes with certain risks, however: the filmmaker can be accused of collaborating with the exploiter; accused of taking advantage of the situation or the characters; and accused of helping construct the situation. Unlike textual ethnography, this discomforting relationship is expansive in that it includes the ethics, methods, and theory in its practice and approach to filming experiential situations and while editing the film. Experiential ethics, then, resides in the textures of touch, the expansiveness of the situation, and the sensible perceptive capacities of the relationship between the filmmaker, the subjects, and the audience as mutual tactile contact (see Chapter 6 in more detail).

The ethics and methods of video ethnography as a practice and a theoretical endeavor do not conform to positivist or measurement-orientated empirical approaches to epistemology and knowledge construction. Instead, video ethnography, as indicated throughout previous chapters, is immersed in experiential situations of ongoing relationships between the filmmaker and the objects and persons within the frame and outside the frame – *the seen and unseen, heard and unheard, the visible and invisible.* Therefore, these situations of empirical experiences embedded in the tactile, sensuous, and self-reflexive relationships require a different ethical, and methodological, and theoretical framework compared to an epistemology of logocentrism or textual epistemologies. To illustrate the ethical and methodological characteristics of video ethnography outlined, I now turn to a detailed examination of a single case study of *Girl Model*.

Girl Model as a case study in video ethnography

Girl Model demonstrates how audiovisual technologies can be integrated into a researcher's methodology in order to help them access and chart fluctuating sensory experiences over time as a mode of ethnographic practice. *Girl Model* traces an extended encounter between Ashley, a 31-year-old American model scout from New York City, and Nadya, a 13-year-old aspiring model from rural Siberia, capturing their interactions as part of an experiential story that engages audiences with sensory immediacy. *Girl Model* merges the dynamics of documentary filmmaking, including the sensibilities of sound, with the methodology of transglobal ethnography to interconnect seemingly disparate nefarious practices in different regions of the world within a political economy of transporting young girls around the world as commodities. It integrates image and sound to provide a cinematic explanation of how and why young Russian teenagers seek fame, notoriety, and income, and how modeling and fashion companies recruit, transport, and exploit these teenage girls. It also demonstrates how lives can be irrevocably marked by encounters that initially seem benign but that turn out to cause harm; in other words, the audience is drawn into an experiential narrative that evokes the everyday realities of human trafficking within a particular ethical framework of experiential participation. Brief encounters between young girls and model scouts become "turning points" in their lives that significantly redirect childhood trajectories and entrap youth within a well-organized, international trafficking industry prefaced on predation. Finally, *Girl Model*'s substance – its "experiential data," in the terms of Campbell (2012) – lies in its findings of lived sensations, which unfold over time.

Girl Model, as a case study, demonstrates how video ethnography or documentary filmmaking can expand researchers' methodological scope and broaden opportunities for knowledge production within current ethical and aesthetic discussions (Sniadecki 2014). The ethics of this particular documentary's narrative help frame and situate Russian modeling culture within a political economy that exploits and fosters the development of a predatory industry built on the sexual and labor exploitation of young girls using tried and tested techniques to lure girls into the industry. The girls and their families' socioeconomic circumstances, in turn, shape the lived experiences of Russian teenage girls and motivate them to enter into this murky industry.

While *Girl Model*'s primary function is to show the real-life experiences of recruitment, transport, and exploitation as a form of experiential aesthetic knowledge within an empirical and sensory narrative, the film also highlights the ambiguous ethical and aesthetic consequences of these experiences in self-reflexive ways. According to Sniadecki (2014, pp. 25–33), by adding self-reflexivity into the movie, video ethnographers integrate themselves into

> methods as a way to respond to the ethical complexities and power dynamics inherent in any act of representation … [it] has the potential to open up intersubjective, experiential forms of knowledge that are shaped by the filmmaker, film-subject, and viewer alike.

In this quote, Sniadecki deliberately merges aesthetics with ethics and the politics of video ethnography with self-reflexivity. Sniadecki's suggestion above invites an open-ended interpretation by an audience that exceeds the ethnographic filmmaker's intentions. Given documentary filmmaking's role in providing open-ended, organic depictions of lived experience, the sensorial knowledge it depicts may produce unintended, or unstable outcomes due to an audience's active involvement in interpreting the project. *Girl Model* offers a clear example of how an emerging documentary filmmaking method-of-attunement embedded within audiovisual frameworks can invite open-ended interpretations.

Problematic ethics and aesthetics of video ethnography

The opening series of images in *Girl Model* depict the reflections and refractions of teenage Russian girls on display for scouts to scrutinize, measure, and recruit. The winter setting is Novosibirsk, a large metropolitan city in the Siberian region of Russia. Hallways and rooms of mirrors reflect infinite images of teenage girls, preparing the audience for the refracted story they're about to enter, while visually and sonically establishing the documentary's larger pattern: exploration of the fusion between flesh, image, and sonic environment. This sequence attempts to bring viewers inside the setting through a series of long-takes and montages that focus on the measurements of the young girls' bodies. Images upon images bleed into each other, blurring the boundaries between real and refracted, fake and original, fiction and nonfiction. The audience is placed inside a simulacrum of images as the film challenges audiences to interpretatively navigate an uncomfortable, transgressive-feeling experiential narrative.

As the scouts evaluate more than 200 bikini-clad girls, criticizing in their presence the size of their hips, the pimples on their adolescent faces, and the need for them to lose weight, the scene transitions to the main scout, Ashley, who is eyeing and photographically studying and recording the film's main character, 13-year-old Nadya, who smiles back at her. It is worth noting that photographic images are reproduced not only within the documentary, but also by the scouts, who photograph hundreds of teenage girls' bodies and faces to enter into their databases. These images and sounds endlessly repeat themselves in the documentary, creating a spectacle of disembodiment. Rather than decoding the meaning of the image, however, the documentary relies on "evoking" experience (Vannini 2015a) to craft sounds and images into extended sensory analysis. Viewers experience the composition of images, colours, tactile interactions, and sounds as a narrative. The documentary combines aesthetical and ethical elements to analyze and explain the recruitment, transport, and exploitation of teenage girls in the Russian modeling industry. At one point, for example, the filmmaker can be seen and heard offering teenage Nadya his phone. This inclusion is deliberately placed in the movie so the audience will understand why and how she obtained the phone to call her mother in Novosibirsk, Russia from Tokyo, Japan.

Girl Model eschews surveys and quantitative analysis about teenagers caught up in the global modeling industry in favor of experiential immersion. This choice may be seen as a response to Back and Puwar's (2013, p. 6) question, "What are the opportunities afforded to researchers where our primary tools are no longer confined to the survey or the tape recorder?" Video ethnography answers that new digital recording technologies, when combined with ethnographic sensibilities and techniques to evoke lived experience, can bring to life dynamic and uncomfortable lived encounters – in this case, encounters between teenage girls and adult scouts. *Girl Model*'s crafting of aesthetic knowledge immerses the audience in uncomfortable situations of sensuousness and spectacle. The film practices immersion and evokes lived experience by directly showing viewers the problematic ethical encounters faced by young girls. This immersion, in turn, allows viewers to perceive the situation from the models' perspective in present-tense time. The audience's understanding of the scene is thus situated within an ethics of the filmmaker's aesthetics that creates a direct connection between audience empathy and the social and political conditions that give rise to these situations.

Framing the scene

Of particular interest here is one scene that serves as an illustration of the ethical and aesthetic themes outlined. Ashley, the film's main scout, is shown wearing her bikini and walking into a bathroom, where she reveals her curious "favourite little spot." She opens a little, white rectangular container and spreads before the camera hundreds of photos of young girls' bodies, feet, and other body parts. Ashley's images are anonymous, cut up, dissected, separated, violated. The objectifying detachment in Ashley's discussion of the photos, and her indifference when she claims to have taken the photos without the girls' consent, reflects her own disconnection to the modeling world in which she works. Ashley's photography raises not only ethical and aesthetic issues, but legal ones, too. Ashley comments on the process of how she obtained her photos:

> So this is my favourite little spot. I had these boxes made for these little mini prints. Stockings. See the hands, gestures. See. I'm trying to hide my camera under the table so they don't know that I am photographing. Sometimes I wouldn't photograph a girl's face, I would just photograph her feet or her hands.

Ashley continues to place photographs of young girls' body parts on the floor. She picks up two separate photographs of two different girls and tries to connect the two fragments as a whole body. She comments on her efforts.

> Sometimes I would try to find the legs. Which legs went with which body? Hey, does that work? That works. Doesn't it? Wait. Oh no, it doesn't work. Wait almost works. This is the same bathing suit though, look. That fits that. I just didn't … if I had it on a tripod then I could …

As her words trail off, the scene transitions into Ashley's admission and explanation of how teenage girls come to be facilitated into prostitution.

What makes the scene ethically ambiguous is how Ashley admits to consciously hiding her camera under tables to photograph up girls' skirts, capturing images of their bodies without permission. As she displays fragmented images of young girls' arms, feet, legs, thighs, and stomachs, it becomes clear to the viewer that not one single photograph shows a young person as a whole body. This scene appeals to video ethnography's ability to evoke lived experience to frame and understand how and why Ashley photographs teenage girls without their consent, why she sifts through hundreds of images of teenage girls, and how she surreptitiously collects images of their body parts as mementos that she stores in a small hidden chest. Yet, the documentary also frames and depicts Ashley's aesthetic actions as ethically ambiguous by demonstrating how her personal behaviour as a scout might be indicative of the larger industry's behaviour (as a corrupt institution that attempts to craft a clean image of itself). *Girl Model* cracks that shiny façade by revealing the hairline fractures through which objectification, recruitment, transport, and exploitation occur. Audiences *feel, hear*, and *see* the substance of these concepts inductively emerging from the narrative of lived experience.

Ethics and aesthetics of video ethnography

It is precisely within the social, political, and personal situations described above that *Girl Model* engages with ethics and aesthetics to address larger themes of video ethnography. Ambiguity and affect delicately play out alongside relationships between "photographer, criminal, victim, spectator, torturer, and artist" in this, and upcoming, scenes. Quoting Levi Strauss (2003, p. 8), Carrabine poses the question, "'What right have I to represent you?' In doing so, the relationship between photographer, suffering subject, and the very act of looking are put at the centre of debate" (Carrabine 2014, pp. 134–158). Aware that these fragmented images will eventually appear in the public domain, *Girl Model* not only bears witness to these processes of dehumanization and exploitation, but it takes things a step further by visually demonstrating the political and economic situations that perpetuate the situation: Ashley's enjoyment at recruiting Russian teenagers, taking their images without consent, and putting them in vulnerable situations is cast within this broader social and ethical light. *Girl Model*, as video ethnography, utilizes audiovisual methods to ethically and aesthetically reframe Ashley's photos by showing the wider networks of organized power that facilitate and encourage her actions. Whether the filmmaker's "intention" meets the audience's "reception" is ambiguous, however. Does an audience see, hear, and interpret the film in the manner that the filmmaker intended?

Here, the role of the audience's subjectivity – viewers' ability to interpret film – is crucial. Dai Vaughan (1999) labels this interpretive process as "ambiguous" in line with my own open-ended approach. Open-ended interpretations complicate attempts to ethically frame photos in just ways. Sniadecki (2014, p. 29) suggests that ambiguity breaks down the binary relationships between ethics/aesthetics and objective/subjective interpretations. Sniadecki cites Vaughan (1999, p. 115):

> just as the ethics of the filmmakers are experienced as aesthetics by the viewer, so the [researcher's] objectivity translates into ambiguity, and the "real-life" density commonly attributed by the viewer to such film is our experience of active engagement in the generation of meaning.

Sniadecki and Vaughan's argument is similar to an open-ended approach in that images and sounds are unruly, dynamic, ambiguous, lacking in linear meaning. In Sniadecki and Vaughan's account, the audience is active rather than passive – a participant in the interpretive creation of audiovisual meaning that extends the experience, rather than a deferential dupe to a predetermined meaning framed and intended by the filmmaker to receive as a message. The open-endedness of images and sounds naturally opens them up to additional, unstable, and indeterminate understandings and interpretations. If open-ended approaches widen and broaden new production and unknown limits to interpretation, then any attempt by the filmmaker to aesthetically and ethically frame images and sounds in just ways become deeply problematic: at any point, the audience can simply strip and reinterpret those intentions. Rather than the stable interpretation intended by the filmmaker, an audience's contact with the slipperiness of a video ethnography or documentary film generates ambiguity. Images and sounds "offer too much" (Sniadecki 2014, p. 29), and, in so doing, may confound efforts to create ethical depictions. Consequently, the filmmaker's intention will always be superseded by the viewer's interpretation. A few implications arise for video ethnography in light of this discussion.

I suggest that documentaries such as *Girl Model* can depict conditions of vulnerability while simultaneously performing ethics as an act of research practice. *Girl Model*'s circulation on iTunes, Netflix, the BBC, PBS, ARTE, news stations, and numerous other outlets has amplified the ambiguities inherent in the film's perspective: is it marking, holding accountable, or promoting the activities depicted? Inasmuch as *Girl Model* functions as an act of ethical practice, irreducible to pre-given "meanings" intended by the filmmaker, it might do all or none of the following: fascinate and humiliate, punish and shame, fetishize and create fascist desire in a field of power. The interpretive possibilities and reactions by audiences are endless, *in spite of the filmmaker's intentions.*

The multidimensionality of audience interpretation of images and sounds, or what audiences bring to the film, can lead to ethical murkiness. Without clear demarcation or explicit signposting, *Girl Model* may not always be interpreted as a film that explores how scouts and the modeling industry exploit the vulnerability of young girls. Will the documentary trouble the conscience and provoke an ethical response? Or will the fragmented images of young girls be seen as aesthetic art that creates affective, fascist, and/or predatory desire, thereby reinforcing the very troublesome behaviours the documentary attempts to critique and highlight? An open-ended framework provides no clear answer to these questions. Carrabine (2014, pp. 134–158) provides a bit more direction when he states, "there is much evidence to suggest that these violations of humanity scarcely trouble consciences." Carrabine also offers a pessimistic illustration of his claim, which can be compared to *Girl Model*: just as the guards at Abu Ghraib appear happy when taking their photos of victims, so Ashley appears proud and satisfied by what she's done to the young girl models and how she's done it with her camera. Even as the documentary attempts to suggest that her aesthetics involve seriously questionable ethical practices, Ashley's own perspective may shine through. She is "not doing these things to fellow human beings, but to those who are no longer quite human" (Carrabine 2014, pp. 134–158). Ashley's collection of images is displayed in front of the documentary filmmaker "as if they were just another sight to be captured along the foreign adventure" (Carrabine 2014, pp. 134–158).

Whether the documentary seizes on this gesture as an ethical moment or positions the gesture as a milder commentary on ethics, fascination, or crude sensationalism are questions influenced by the subjectivity of the viewer and what they bring to the film, how the ambiguity of images and sounds are received, and the degree to which the framework of intentions constructed by the filmmaker are legible or explicit. Perhaps audiences' ability to empathize or to feel protective of teenage girls also comes into play. Ethical analysis of such factors lie at the heart of video ethnography, with its focus on the nuances of interpretation mediated through culture, lived experience, subjectivity, and normative approaches. *Girl Model* doesn't explicitly identify the industry's actions, or Ashley's, as criminal, or condemn them; but it does frame them as ethically questionable, transgressive, harmful, and possibly illegal. It raises questions without providing answers: Are the girls victims of crimes? Are the photographs visual evidence of vulnerability, abuse of power, and criminal behaviour? *Girl Model* belongs to a space of messy ethical aesthetics rather than in the more comfortable realm of stable interpretations with definite ethical answers. Audiences can easily interpret evidence as aesthetics, and aesthetics as evidence.

Conclusion: theoretical and methodological implications

At least three conclusions can be drawn from the process of integrating video ethnography into research as a viable and legitimate mode of experiential sensory inquiry. First, images and sounds of lived experience play out in real time as active moments, and this very fluidity gives their sensory and temporal qualities an edge when compared to written research. Video ethnography is also multidimensional, incorporating evocative images, videos, archival footage, and sounds of lived experiences from several angles. In the case of *Girl Model*, these angles are many and diverse, ranging from the experiences of the scouts, to teenage girls, the filmmakers, the owners of the modeling companies, the audiences of the film, and the readers of reviews and studies of the film. Audiences are engaged with experiential, unfolding indeterminate scenes and encouraged to synthesize them, imbuing them with their own interpretation.

Second, video ethnography expands audiovisual methods into the realm of *evoking lived experience* as a form of aesthetic analysis. Video ethnography does this by carefully evoking everyday textures of lived experience. For example, *Girl Model* uses video methods to analyze and depict the process by which aspiring Russian models are recruited, transported, and exploited – the foundational criteria of human trafficking. This position overlaps with Jefferies' (2013, p. 315) explanation that documentary filmmaking functions as an aesthetic intervention that

> evokes a central question for artists and filmmakers trying to intervene politically in sites of collective anguish: what can art *do* and what can it *become* in its relation with the lived experience of traumatic events? [Documentary's] aesthetic strategy, together with its inventive approach to exhibition and circulation, aims to

provoke a public reckoning with the confusion and pain wrought by both the crimes and the dominant narratives of responsibilization and individualization.

Jefferies (2013) discusses how the documentary *Señorita Extraviada* reappropriates representational space from state and commercial media; in a similar fashion, *Girl Model* reappropriates representational space from the modeling and fashion realm, customarily delivered through reality TV shows such as *America's Next Top Model, Models Inc., Top Model, I Wanna Be a Model, The Face, Make Me a Supermodel*, and others. Because the methods of dissemination and stylistic approaches used in video ethnography are quite different from those used in traditional written scholarly work, video ethnography offers the opportunity for scholars to reach publics who would not otherwise read a scholarly article.

Third, video ethnography allows researchers to craft images and sounds out of lived experiences to produce what MacDougall calls the "production of experiences as knowledge" (see MacDougall 2006; Sniadecki 2014), or sensory experience. Scholarly emphasis on sensory experience fosters a sensory response to lived experience so that audiences become immersed in the sonic and visual elements of the documentary film, and experience political and economic, animal, and "other" lived experience in direct, visceral ways. Video ethnography reimagines "findings" using sound, colour, texture, gestures, images, and speech. When making video ethnographies filmmakers use their own senses and technology to interpret sensory experience, a process that is often further complicated by audiences, who bring their own understandings and interpretations to the layers of open-ended arranged sensory material.

While video ethnography draws on sensory studies to explore the intersection of cultural texts, sociopolitical contexts, and lived experience (Jefferies 2013, p. 306), it also borrows from documentary filmmaking techniques, practices, and ideas to create a novel approach to understanding and analyzing lived experiences. An implication of this methodological transition is a shift in the way that knowledge is crafted, disseminated, and shared: in the 20th century, knowledge was most often communicated verbally, or in written form; in the 21st century, knowledge depiction is taking a sensory, iconic, and sonic turn that focuses on digital transmission through and to the senses.

Note

1 Readers can access *Girl Model* at https://vimeo.com/29694894 with the password *industry*.

6

FILM FESTIVALS, THE PUBLIC SPHERE, AND THE ETHICS OF VIDEO ETHNOGRAPHY

Kamp Katrina as a case study

Earlier in this book I suggested that video ethnography surpasses the capacity of written textual publications to depict lived experience because of video ethnography's brute, wild, and vital properties and because of its ability to foster experiential sensory knowledge. I have discussed in detail the advantages and limitations of video ethnography, making my case for its strength as an experiential means of understanding lived experience, falling somewhere between art and ethnography, neither conforming to strict cinema verité or conventional mainstream documentary practices, nor constrained by traditional ethnographic film, abandoning titles, signposting, explanation, voice-over, etc. I have described how expressive encounters grounded in perceptive, felt, gestural, and "of the moment" treatment, thanks to the fluidity and spontaneity of the video medium, allow for a tactile and interactive practice that complements and even exceeds descriptive prose, communicating sensory aspects reflecting the dynamic flux of experiences in ways that allow researchers and scholars a vital means of depicting and analyzing social life.

Video ethnography offers exciting opportunities to expand the depiction of experiences in a sensory direction, using affective media to augment the current practice of interpreting culture using written prose, stills, and contextualizing explanation. Video ethnography ushers in the possibility of cinematically evoking lived experience and the promise of bringing researchers into an experience of immediacy and intimacy in which they are more easily able to physically attune to sensory details in the field through physical proximity or immersion. Video ethnography turns its lenses and sound recorders toward vibrant materiality in the form of humans, nonhumans, landscapes, seascapes, environments, objects, sounds, and bodies – sometimes completely without orientating texts or the spoken word. Audiences are immersed in and witness these experiences in ways that intensify an understanding of society, but also in ways that bring their own experiences into play as their viewing shapes the interpretation and ethics of the cinematic experience.

In this final chapter I want to elaborate more on the audience experience, the ethics of video documentary, and on the distribution spaces and contexts in which video ethnographies are screened: at film festivals in the public sphere and on digital platforms in audiences' homes. I will conclude this book with a discussion of ethics and the interpretative flux and instability of video ethnographies when they circulate as artworks in the wider world beyond scholarly institutions. I will do so with an extensive discussion on these ethics with a case study on *Kamp Katrina*, a documentary I codirected with my partner Ashley Sabin.

Film festivals and the public sphere

Unlike academic conferences or journal articles, film festivals are not overtly scholarly and those who attend are generally not scholars. Film festivals are film and local community events that open up public venues for screening media, often with post-screening questions and responses from the public involving the live or Skyped, in the presence of directors. These festivals are a chance for audiences to reflect on films as they watch them, and to potentially hear directly from the filmmakers, posing questions to them about their methodology and process. In this regard, although not scholarly, film festivals are process-orientated. Most festivals include media workshops that focus on the production process, techniques, stylistic orientations, and skills, even offering consultation, lectures, and hands-on retreats to more deeply discuss how directors, producers, and editors shape stories, with public discussions, forums, and even debates about the ethics of practice, issues such as voice, power, and diversity, etc. Film festivals create publics for people who are drawn to film as an expressive art form – including festival organizers and volunteers; sponsors; and an industry of people who sell and license nonfiction films. During film festivals, publics respond to curated films by reviewing them and sharing ideas about them in person, by word of mouth and through social media forums, and by participating in competitions and forums set up by the festival, for example voting on the "best" film, question and answer discussions, interviews with directors, and online video critiques. Film festival audiences also respond physically, viscerally, and emotionally to the films they see within the movie theatre space: clapping, laughing, and through discussions with other audience members after the film has screened. The films screened are often international in scope and embody a diverse global community. A film festival is thus a temporary and recurring physical place in the public sphere that offers a wide public (as long as entrance fees are affordable) a chance to encounter a range of films, including ethnographic. Film festivals provide a place where organizers, filmmakers, and public communities can meet to interact in physically present ways, and foster an inclusive spirit whereby non-scholarly and nonprofessional views are included within the sphere of scholars, critics, buyers, judges, and professional mentors and exemplary role models.

Often sponsored by local commercial entities and through city and state grants, film festivals help cultivate a public sphere in which documentary films and video ethnographies become celebrated artworks. The space and culture and experience of any given film festival makes for a potential subject for video ethnography itself to explore, evoke, and communicate as a lived experience. Film festivals can feel vibrant and catalyzing, not only to the filmmakers who participate and who find new enthusiasm and audiences for their works, but for audiences who mingle in a live, vital space with other enthusiasts to discuss aesthetic possibilities. Ivakhiv (2013, p. 87) suggests that we live in an age of motion picture and those motions of pictures radically alter our sense of relationship with technology, films, and each other. "Relational processes and events – those activities and encounters by which things emerge, grow, interact, and affect the world around them – are central, and objects, including films, are considered not so much for what they *are* for what they *do*" (2013, pp. 63–87, original italics). Video ethnographies, as circulating lived experiences, join this flow of symbolic systems of interpretation (film festivals), and engage public spheres as more than simply commodities but also as cultural artifacts that are discussed, face-to-face, in throngs, and crowds, and groups. These features "can be thought of as the interrelations that make up what Merleau-Ponty described as the fleshy, interpenetrating chiasmus of self and world" (1965, p. 91).

Likewise, Vannini (2015a) has indicated how ethnographic documentaries are increasingly garnering attention in the public sphere thanks to the growth and presence of film festivals and digital platforms. In other words, alongside the rise of researchers' scholarly training and use of video ethnography as a means of expressive exploration and analysis of lived experience, we have witnessed the rise of a new emphasis within the film festival sphere on "cultural documentaries," or ethnographic experiences, including relatively advanced public discussions of ethical considerations, as part of the film festival experience.

Film festivals most certainly help to introduce new forms of knowledge into the public sphere, albeit in a commodified form of knowledge that, as Habermas (1991) notes, is responded to in the form of taste and preferences, and even "markets." Nevertheless, video ethnographies are more than simply commodities and when they are presented publicly they do much to fuse and forge connections between scholarly worlds and public worlds and between worlds of all kinds, for example, between the shepherds of *Sweetgrass* or the fishermen of *Leviathan* or the donkeys of *Sanctuary*, and urban film festival audiences. When they are presented in the public sphere, video ethnographies can bridge the gap between the private and the public; they can cross disciplinary boundaries (social anthropology and art, for example), foster sensitivity to differences, "soften" hardened stances toward the "other," and proliferate multiple discourses – political, class-based, interspecies, cultural, sociological, aesthetic – that arise from the material conditions of sensuous experience. Video ethnographies can help lead audiences into critical thinking and can help scholars to reflect on the limitations and constraints of conventional forms of academic knowledge – perhaps even acknowledging the flatness of written textual knowledge compared to the plentitude and vitality of video ethnography's distinctive sensuous knowledge. Personally, I regard video ethnographies as on an equal footing to scholarly books or peer-reviewed articles that actively shape and reflect concerns and analysis about social and public life. When filmmakers immersively plunge into other worlds and relate these worlds in sensuous ways, they do not need to be scholars, in any formal sense, to be contributors to scholarship. When such works are seen and discussed publicly in film festivals, they take on an added vitality, thick with audience responses, brute and wild feedback and response, sometimes caught in question and answer sessions that are videotaped, and so on. Film festivals play a crucial role in contributing to the creation of the public sphere where the ethics of the filmmaker and the themes of the film are central concerns of viewers.

Screening video ethnographies at film festivals is also crucial for their reach and ability to spark discussion, at a time when textual knowledge – lectures, articles, and books – continues to dominate institutional scholarly environments. Video ethnographies not only circulate in non-scholarly public domains such as film festivals, but also serve to blur interdisciplinary boundaries, helping to advance intersectional interdisciplinary concerns, while helping to foster public-facing forums for scholarly and public ethnography. Currently the active, engaged, and open-ended framework of film festivals helps to provide spaces that counter the dominance of academia's textually-based forms and mediums of knowledge.

Importantly, unlike textual publications where the ethics of the research is clearly delineated and partitioned into different written sections of the article, ethnographic films do not function in a linear method or unfold with caveats about their methodology. Instead, the ethics of the film arise from and are embedded in their nonlinear, immersive aesthetics and within the very practice of making the film. Therefore, two key questions I want to pose in concluding this book are: (1) What alternative role to conventional academic knowledge (printed, written) can video ethnographies and the film festivals that support their circulation play in the public sphere? (2) What questions or implications for this public sphere and its functioning as an interpretative space may arise from the inherent ethical ambiguities or interpretative instability of video ethnography as discussed in the previous chapter's consideration of the possibilities of reception of *Girl Model*? I will respond to both these questions by drawing on ideas, observations, and thoughts raised in previous chapters of this book in order to more fully consider the role of the film festival and the public sphere as an underexplored component or facet of video ethnography.

If film festivals open up a participatory public forum for discussions of media, human rights, social action, and discussions of filmmaking ethics then video ethnographers presenting their films to the public at such film festivals are inevitably involved in such public forums, however scholarly their training. I believe that film festivals are contemporary forums that resemble Habermas' notion of the public sphere (e.g., coffee shops and clubs) and Brophy's (1997) discussion of the rise of plebeian festivals. Films, when screened in festivals, can offer the possibility of political participation of marginalized groups alongside dominant ones. They can mix up and diversify audiences for "art" and ethnography alike. Unlike scholarly articles, or reading groups, films can draw sizeable audiences, attracting multiple groups of people to the public sphere where multiple viewpoints and subjectivities are brought into play.

By arguing for the social good of releasing video ethnographies at film festivals, I do not intend to undermine social science's role in public life or to suggest that video ethnographies replace more conventional forms of social science research and publication. Instead, I see video ethnographies as meaningful extensions of social science that tell stories within larger social narratives and that draw more generalized and diverse publics toward social science research, ideas, and practices. Video ethnographies can meaningfully engage with social concerns, respond to real events as praxis, and participate in local and international publics that engage people visually, sonically, and discursively. They can also help introduce ideas and studies from the social sciences into the wider public sphere, serving as ambassadors for the discipline as a whole. The presence of video ethnographies at film festivals can help to expand and redefine what counts as legitimate academic knowledge. It also means that video ethnographies can extend beyond "the ivory tower" to participate in and help shape cultural, civic, and social life. Film festivals circumvent the logocentric and textual bias of academia and extend scholarly ideas and research into the public sphere by means of video ethnographies.

Currently, little has been studied or written regarding the relationship between film festivals, video ethnographies, and the public sphere. For this reason I look back to Habermas (1991) who has addressed festivals and the media in his analysis of the transformation of the public sphere (while never writing about the role of film festivals directly). Habermas (1991) notes that festivals had lost their public character by the 18th century because they moved from the public streets into the rooms of the private palaces, which resulted in the partial exclusion of plebeians who used their bodies to celebrate in public. When festivals were staged by the bourgeois, they "served not so much the pleasure of the participants as the demonstration of grandeur" (Habermas 1991). Plebeians, however, countered this status-driven conspicuous display of "grandeur" with their own style of festivity by returning to the streets to celebrate, despite the bourgeoisie's attempt to remove festivals from the public sphere. This accompanied the emergence of an aristocratic society that separated itself from the state. Habermas (1991) notes that the banquets of bourgeois notables became exclusive, taking place in the private sphere behind closed doors. I note that, today, film festivals can also function in a similar way, especially when priced beyond the reach of ordinary local publics.

Habermas believes that this transition of festivals from the public streets into the private rooms of the bourgeois home led to the *first* separation of the private and public sphere in a specifically modern sense. Habermas then turns his attention to issues concerning the emergence of bourgeois civil society and its eventual decline. I note that Habermas does not analyze in any great detail what concurrently happened among common people and how they used festivals to gain legitimacy and form countercultures in the public sphere. I also note that Habermas tends to privilege rationality and reason, while ignoring the haptic sphere of sensation, images, sounds, and the body, when he characterizes the public sphere. Habermas overlooks the significance of the affective, the expressively depicted, and the expressive dimensions of the public sphere, all of which are significant components of film festivals – albeit often located inside commodified, specialized, high-dollar, and privatized spaces that are not always open to the public. Because Habermas devotes scant attention to how street festivals developed, were almost eliminated, and then were eventually revived in the public sphere by the plebeians, and how these transformations occurred, his scholarship ignores possibilities, such as that many of today's festivals are affective, street-level, direct responses to the rationalization and privatization of festivals Habermas describes. While for Habermas the emotional and affective or bodily aspects of street festivals are aspects he considers irrational and antimodern, detracting from the rational goal of emancipation, for me, and other scholars, festivals that are public, street level and affective are fascinating sites of aesthetic experience and experiential, haptic sensory knowledge.

Because Habermas is more interested in communicative rationality and emancipation than in the value of the sensory, visual, and sonic domain, his account of festivals cannot easily be applied to film festivals which are entirely based around a sensuous art form that uses sensory images and sounds rather than textual or written, discursive analysis and knowledge.

Brophy (1997, p. 878) illustrates how, in Germany, festivals functioned as mediums "for reflecting on the general rules governing social relations." Instead of the feared outcomes of violence and revolution, plebeian festival societies used humor, emotion, satire, and ridicule to contest the bounds of censorship, restrictions, religious customs, and order set forth by bourgeois civil society. For example, speakers in the public sphere during festivals "were given a wide range of latitude to criticize issues and behave in ways that transgressed accepted social and political norms" (Brophy 1997, p. 879). These plebeian festival societies enhanced the public sphere in two ways. First, the performance of satire and ridicule forced citizens to reflect critically on social relations. Second, its oral form emphasized bourgeois ideas to circulate throughout the public sphere and transfer to "artisanal and laboring circles, which were ... simply less welcome in bourgeois clubs and lodges" (Brophy 1997, p. 879).

Brophy's discussion of festivals and the public sphere merits attention. First, plebeians created a social space within the public sphere that paved the way for alternative countercultures to emerge against bourgeois civil society (Brophy 1997). Second, the humor and emotions of this social space helped carve out a niche in the public sphere through which plebeians were able to establish an identity to counter bourgeois identity. Third, and perhaps most importantly, attaining social space during festivals provided plebeians with a platform and a sense of common purpose that helped them to organize themselves in a public space. In other words, the public space plebeians carved out during festivals helped generate a sense of shared and common purpose to unify, socially coalesce, and refashion what was previously a wholly bourgeois street culture. From this point forward (1825–1830), a street culture emerged as a spontaneous gathering place during festivals.

However, just as Habermas' characterization of festivals overlooks the role of the sensory, so Brophy's (1997) focus on plebeians and class also neglects to discuss the role of the body and sensory knowledge in his analysis and theory of festival history. In class terms, if sensory knowledge is the underclass that continues to be overlooked within contemporary bourgeois academic culture, then film festivals, much as Brophy described plebeian festivals doing, help to carve out a niche or counter space for the plebeian or sensory form of knowledge. In other words, film festivals share some of the same qualities as Brophy's plebeian festivals because they foreground films, or sensory knowledge, as a subaltern public sphere and help forge a more grassroots or street space in which video ethnographies are able to be seen and discussed, and influence cultural and social life in sensory ways as a sensory aesthetic form of knowledge.

I define film festivals as subaltern public spheres for video ethnographies because festivals help create publics in civil society that center around screening a variety of films, with the participatory role of audiences, festival organizers, volunteers, and sponsors, and an industry of people who sell and license nonfiction films. Film festivals encourage public debate about social life and aesthetics through the creation of affective spaces in screening rooms as films mediate and affect audiences.

Marks (2000, p. 16) argues that films and videos are "produced within a large network of sites, including media access centers, colleges and universities, public television stations, cable access programs, and of course garage and bedroom studios." But in general I find that little attention is given to where these video ethnographies go after they are produced, or, in other words, the life they go on to lead and their influence as circulating media, shaping responses, discourse, and even the production of other films in response. This question would never be posed for written forms of scholarship, the dominant form. Academic journals exist for the publication of textually-based knowledge, but the majority of journals have not yet expanded to include online video publications, although, according to Vannini (2015a), they are rapidly moving in this direction. But until there is more disseminating and distributive space for video ethnographies, the lack of journals with online video publications means that most video ethnographers who want to disseminate their work face a serious obstacle and no alternative but to turn to film festivals. The lack of space made within academia for video ethnographies, serves to undermine them as a legitimate form of scholarly knowledge that deserves to be considered alongside written scholarship. It poses serious problems for the work making the light of day, getting viewed, discussed, and woven into critical and scholarly responses. "Once the work is made, intercultural film/videomakers have a great challenge to distribute and exhibit it" (Marks 2000, p. 17).

One of the advantages of being forced to go beyond the realm of academic publishing is that researchers who produce video ethnographies, who are forced to approach video and film distributors as well as film festivals, in order to disseminate their video ethnographies, are more easily able to cross from the scholarly into the public sphere. In this sphere they will

> deal with festivals, galleries and museums, and academic bookers, with management styles ranging from actively marketing film/video packages to complete laissez-faire ... It is at the live events that one can see the audience that has been constituted around this work, and this is a thrilling event that the circumstances of virtual audiences just don't permit.
>
> *Marks 2000, pp. 17–18*

Video and film distributors circulate films internationally to a variety of locations,

> from local broadcast to college lecture room, from community hall to art museum, from a screening for the maker's family and friends to an artist-run center. Each viewing expands the meaning of a work; as reception theorists say, it completes it ... Their very circulation is a kind of coalition building, reinforced by networks both ephemeral and concrete, from gossip and email to community organizations, university classes, and funding agencies.
>
> *Marks 2000, pp. 19–21*

Following Marks' (2000, p. 80) argument, video ethnographies bind with audiences to build both a distributive infrastructure and an expansion of the video ethnography's meaning through the variety of different kinds of audience screenings. For example, a film like *Girl Model* might be screened to teenage girls and models, students, feminist groups, and sex trafficking-prevention activists, as well as to social scientists.

Film festivals form part of this expansion of meaning as part of this infrastructure or ecology of distribution:

> From production and distribution to consumption and recirculation, the cinematic experience is inescapably embedded in ecological webs. Cinematic texts, with their audiovisual presentations of individuals and their habitats, affect our imaginations of the world around us, and thus, potentially, our actions toward this world.
>
> *Rust et al., 2013, p. 2*

Film festivals as public ethnography

If by definition a public is a group of physical bodies experiencing films as sensory aesthetic knowledge through their bodies then,

> How can communication proceed when many members are non-linguistic? Can we theorize more closely the various forms of such communicative energies? How can humans learn to hear or enhance our receptivity to propositions not expressed in words? What kind of institutions and rituals of democracy would be appropriate?
>
> *Bennett 2009, p. 104*

Bennett's ideas about vibrant materiality in the form of humans, nonhumans, sounds, and bodies can be applied to film festivals as sites of sensuous vibrant public participation that decentralize and circulate moving images and sounds as a form of public ethnography (Vannini 2015a).

Public ethnography asks several questions, such as, what is the relationship between ethnographic knowledge and the public? What does knowledge do? What counts as knowledge? Which gatekeepers – editors, publishers, producers – decide to include ethnographical knowledge in the public domain? Michael Burawoy, Herbert Gans, and Phillip Vannini have all contributed to the development of public ethnography. According to Burawoy (2000), sociology is largely divided between professional and public knowledge. Professional knowledge can be characterized as empirical data, academic conferences, and specialized language, sometimes known as "jargon," that is often disconnected from the public sphere. Burawoy characterizes public knowledge as empirical inquiry with policy orientations, knowledge that is concerned with the collective good, and a connection from the production of knowledge that is reflexive and morally driven. He suggests that public sociology should be written in ways that allow nonsociologists to understand the language; he recommends a storytelling approach with nontechnical language that feels accessible and relevant to any nonspecialist public.

Gans (2010) echoes many of the same ideas as Burawoy. Gans urges for more of the kind of ethnography that might become part of the public sphere. "This requires more sociological research and other writing of relevance to the larger world beyond sociology and in all the corners of the discipline" (Gans 2010, p. 98). A goal of public ethnography, according to Gans, is to make the discipline more publicly useful instead of academically insular. Ethnographers often go behind the scenes, behind the scenes of peoples' lives, to understand the nuances of challenges they face, or social ills, and to explore how everyday lives and networks are organized. A successful public ethnography, for Gans, is one that allows the public to have a better understanding of the experiences of people who, for example, might encounter social problems, or ways to better show how institutions work. Gans also mentions the importance of utilizing audio and video in the presentation and delivering of public ethnography. "Magazine articles, radio and TV documentaries and their digital equivalents go through a roughly similar gatekeeping process" (Gans 2010, p. 101). Radio stations and TV might be places to disseminate video ethnographies, but video ethnographers are often reluctant to broadcast their work for fear of violating ethical professional standards. I believe that Gans' strength lies in his explicit advocacy of public ethnography and the concrete recommendations he makes about where an interface with the public might be found; however, I note that Gans stops short of suggesting how to implement this kind of public availability. To find a more pragmatic set of suggestions for making public ethnography available, I will now turn to Vannini.

Vannini's *Innovative Ethnographies* series is one of the first long-form projects to take seriously thought, practice, and dissemination of public ethnography.[1] One of Vannini's goal is to popularize research (see popularizing research), in order to communicate with wider audiences beyond academia. In his words,

> I decided to cut to the chase and promised to deliver a book for the bored and disenfranchised, for those feeling alienated from the drudgery of academic writing and inauthentic about producing more of the same drivel, and for those willing to let their academic imagination play.[2]

Within a matter of days, Vannini received numerous submissions along with academics congratulating him on his pursuit of communicating with people outside of academia. Public ethnography brings social science research into a "conversation with publics, understood as people who are themselves involved in a conversation."[3]

Vannini (2015a) decided to expand his interest beyond writing, to make a video ethnography (see *Life Off Grid* and *Off the Grid*) and disseminate it through film festivals and online media. Vannini (2015a) has indicated how ethnographic documentaries are increasingly garnering attention in the public sphere. No longer reliant on professional knowledge, theoretical training, or methodological instruction, popular ethnographers have turned to Netflix, iTunes, TV, film festivals, museums, galleries, and other modes of dissemination of their ethnographic movies. The majority of these popular DIY ethnographies, he suggests, have "superior evocative, narrative, sensuous, performative, and attention-grabbing qualities" (Vannini 2015a) and therefore bring ethnographic knowledge into the public sphere while actively shaping public and private lives. These films often play in the public sphere as part of film festivals, leading me to raise some ethical concerns and challenges about their reception and practice.

Ethical challenges

I will now discuss some ethical challenges that characterize the release of popular video ethnographies in the context of public or popular sociology. The film festival is where the film and its audience meet each other for the first time – and it is in this moment that programmers, critics, audiences, journalists, and academics must negotiate a set of inevitable ethics regarding the representation of subjects in their film work.

My reason for raising these concerns is motivated by my desire to guide researchers making video ethnographies in anticipating and understanding the kinds of ethically complex situations they may encounter after their film's public release. Some of these situations arise at the production stage of the film. For example, it is not unusual for filmmakers to get caught up in criminal activities or to be shot at (*Harlan County, USA*), get shot (*Death in Gaza, Stranger with a Camera*), or reenact mass murders and genocide on camera (*The Act of Killing*). Adler (1993, p. 23) explains that field researchers who study marginal activities

> must inevitably break the law in order to acquire valid participant observation data. This occurs in its most innocuous form from having "guilty knowledge": information about crimes that are committed ... and by being present at the scene of a crime and witnessing its occurrence.

Owing to a lack of written studies about the experience of video ethnographers conducting research on ethically difficult circumstances and subjects while making a video ethnography, and because very few video ethnographers are prone to discuss their research relationships, I would like to address this vacuum by asking the following questions: What should video ethnographers who conduct research on ethically problematic situations expect to encounter? How do video ethnographers legitimately carry out research on ethically ambiguous behaviors and how can they explain or justify filmmaking practices that violate the law? In the words of Ferrell and Hamm (1998, p. 241), my questions "bring increased attention to ethical challenges that academic professionals have largely ignored in the past." The challenge becomes negotiating ethical codes while conducting research in areas of high risk or as issues arise unexpectedly during filming.

We can begin to address these questions by taking into account an article published by Erich Goode (1999) in which she discusses a dilemma: how can researchers who become involved with their informants pretend that they have no self, or imagine that their embodied and subjective experiences are somehow not relevant to their research?

"To specify the matter a bit," Goode writes,

> for the most part sociological and anthropological researchers have been remarkably coy about ... their personal experiences, what does not get written about in their research reports, what goes on behind closed doors, their unauthorized experiences – experiences they are not permitted, whether by informal social convention or professional decree, to discuss; even more important, experiences that, were they to violate these rules, most of their peers would feel they should not have had in the first place ... The fact is,

we are not being given the full story on the actual participation of most social science observers in the behaviors they examine and involvements with the people they study. By that I mean that there is almost certainly a great deal more participation and involvement that is admitted; full self-disclosure tends to be the exception rather than the rule.

Goode 1999, p. 302

I agree with Goode in that, for the most part, researchers rarely, if at all, disclose their experiences or the complex negotiations they must make ethically while conducting research, or how those experiences influence, shape, and feed into the outcome of their project. Video ethnography adopts a very different approach to this dilemma, because it habitually incorporates ethically ambiguous or ethically challenging situations using a self-reflexive approach that allows audiences to consider the filmmaker's role and presence in the film as they watch.

Today's media-saturated environment has led to the continuous presence of cameras in everyday routines – at home, at work, at airports, parks, and/or in neighborhoods. It is worth noting that ethical guidelines in the British and American Sociology Associations have not been updated to address the ubiquitous presence of video cameras. The Associations' published set of guidelines are based on past attempts to preserve anonymity and confidentiality. While sometimes these goals can be achieved in video ethnography – and are often important – most anonymity and confidentiality issues seem to me to be largely irrelevant. The majority of people I film want their faces and voices seen and heard, not concealed, erased/pixilated, or made invisible. The camera and sound recorder provide an opportunity to show the difficulties of their situation and for their voices to be heard. Video ethnographies allow their worlds to be represented and seen. Additionally, since June 2018, the American Sociology Association's code of ethics has added only one, and one very problematic sentence, on the use of video cameras:

> 11.5 Use of Recording Technology. Sociologists obtain informed consent from research participants, colleagues, students, employees, clients, or others prior to photographing, videotaping, filming, or recording them in any form, unless these activities involve naturalistic observations in public places where confidentiality is not expected and it is not anticipated that the recording will be used in a manner that could cause personal identification or harm.

Nowhere does this code of conduct specify the definition of a "public place," "naturalistic observation," or the definition of "harm." "Naturalistic observation" strikes me as particularly risible because video cameras never simply observe but inherently have a point of view, a motivation, and construct and evoke experiential moments. Filmmakers do not "naturally" or even casually record experiences as detached, objective observers, nor is a filmmaker ever neutral or without some kind of inherent bias. And while receiving and giving informed consent is understandable, it is not realistic or even logistically possible to promise that harm will or will not occur given the unknown outcomes of releasing a film into the public sphere.

The British Sociology Association's two sentences on the use of video cameras are similarly inadequate:

> Research participants should understand how far they will be afforded anonymity and confidentiality and should be able to reject the use of data gathering devices such as tape recorders and video cameras. Anonymity can also be compromised by the use of photographs and, particularly, online platforms and social media.

Researchers who conduct fieldwork on marginal behaviors and activities that violate the law can benefit from a degree of conceptual guidance prior to beginning to conducting research with a camera. Better still, they might turn to *Ethnography at the Edge* whose editors Ferrell and Hamm (1998, p. 243), propose that,

> at minimum, decisions about participating in illegal acts should be made with reference to a hierarchy of consequences that would classify, in general terms, the moral consequences of various types of behavior. At the top of this hierarchy are illegal acts that lead unambiguously to the harming of others, in either physical or psychological sense. So, for example, we could say that a researcher even tangentially involved in street crime is engaging in unethical behavior. At the other end of the continuum are illegal acts that clearly do not injure others and may contribute to a political/moral agenda that the researcher embraces.

A researcher's direct or indirect involvement when filming people's actions that violate laws can be characterized as wholly about ethics. Here, the idea of situational ethics is key, given that when filming, situations can rapidly arise, evolve, or change, leading to circumstances in which researchers suddenly, and often unexpectedly, find themselves facing ethical dilemmas they must negotiate with flexibility. Recording ethically challenging activities and including them in the final version of the film seems to me to be one way to, at the very least, show explicitly that ethical conundrums routinely occur *as part of any given research process and should be included in the film*. Ethical boundaries are muddy, messy, and personal. They are not easy to apprehend or to pinpoint while in the moment of filming, much as in life ethical conundrums arise in often unexpected ways. I believe that such muddled moments should be included in video ethnography as part of the narrative and as a way of honestly reflecting the complexity of making the video.

I also believe that video ethnographers should choose to discuss the potential for ethically challenging situations to arise prior to interviewing or filming people before they appear in ethically dubious or illegal situations, or before a video ethnographer accidentally encounters them. People who appear in the film will therefore be more likely to feel empowered to ask the filmmaker to stop recording or to put down the camera at such moments. Again, these moments of asking for the camera to be shut off – including those that break the law – can be included in the final version of the film to illustrate what is off-limits, what can be seen, and what cannot be seen and heard, thereby demonstrating to the audience that what they are watching and hearing is only a partial experience of a much wider and more complex situation – one in which the filmmaker and subjects actively co-create. This practice also demonstrates the complexity of wider contexts in which such situations arise and through which such behaviors occur. Therefore, it is important, as Becker (1999, pp. 107–108) indicates, to select as many diverse experiences as possible to enhance the interpretation of a film – including illegal actions as well as ethically dubious ones.

> Treating the full range of cases, then, means including what we might otherwise leave out as in some way too weird or raunchy for proper sociologists to consider. It also means using such cases to define and point to the other end of the scale, those activities that are too good to be true, the angelic deviations ... This often takes the form of comparisons that seem shocking or highly improper ... Leaving cases out because they seem tasteless or politically discomforting is equally guaranteed to be a mistake. Good taste is a potent form of social control. Nothing is easier than to get someone to stop doing something we don't like by suggesting that it is "cheap" or "not cool" or "gauche" or any of a hundred similar put-downs. The Russian literary critic Bakhtin pointed out that Rabelais told his tales of Gargantua's carryings on in common vulgar language precisely because it was politically offensive to the educated folk who would have preferred a "more elevated" tone. We are likely to be responding to someone's exercise of social control when we unthinkingly accept such criticism, and social scientists often do.

Including moments that subjects might not want in the movie raises a number of ethical questions while also giving attention to the responsibility carried by the video ethnographer at the point when the film goes "public," or enters the public sphere. How does the filmmaker decide what to omit and what to include when thinking through ethically dubious and/or illegal acts in the film? Examples might include corporate corruption, human trafficking, people who abuse animals, and many more. My own position is that video ethnographers should include as much ethically complex visual and sonic material as necessary in order to do full justice to the complexity of those experiences being filmed, recorded, and/or evoked. I believe that video ethnography's experiential approach to ethics grounds all decision-making about the scope of filming in an understanding of the messy aesthetics of many situations in which the stakes of the ethical or illegal context run high. By including ethically dubious or criminal action in a film, the audience is called upon to actively interpret and reflect upon the complexities of the ethical situation in which the filmmaker made the film, thereby immersively experiencing the situation in its "wild" state. The video ethnographer's only responsibility is to fully articulate the complexities of the situation as immersively as possible for viewers, by putting them in the experiential situation – even if the material is gauche, ugly, dirty, illegal, or difficult to watch and hear, it is crucial to give audiences every chance to appreciate the intricacy, complexity, and ambiguity of ethical situations arising. I believe that this is what separates a rhetorical piece of media from a video ethnography and that only by giving space and time to the full complexity of experiential situations filmed, can meaningful conversations occur in the public sphere. In other words, video ethnography challenges audiences to develop their own interpretive skills and reasoning, and to adopt a more situational ethics-based set of responses. As so many audiences are exposed to other forms of media that paint reductive, black and white pictures of the world, video ethnography can play a key role in opening audiences up to the vagaries and intricacies of real-world experience, its muddiness, and allow them to experience their own interpretative skill instead of being on the receiving end of sanitized storytelling that treats audiences as consumers who want a story that has a clear moral viewpoint and outcome.

From my own experience of making video ethnographies, I can avow that ethical considerations and complexities can feel personally taxing and challenging yet can also present opportunities for growth as a researcher and for the development of resilience and capacity for complexity in both filmmakers and audiences alike. In order to illustrate this idea of the benefits of situational ethics, flexibility, and personal thoughtfulness and honesty when making video ethnographies, I would like to conclude with a case study of my experience of making the documentary film *Kamp Katrina*, a film that plunged my filmmaking partner Ashley Sabin and I into a series of ethical challenges and negotiations that I believe can be usefully shared.

Kamp Katrina: a case study of video ethnography, ethics, and the public sphere

My collaborator Ashley Sabin and I made *Kamp Katrina* together in 2005 and 2006. In order to make the film we relocated to post-Katrina New Orleans immediately after the disastrous flood and remained immersed in daily post-flooded life on the ground in recovering New Orleans for one year. Some of the time we stayed in the home of Ms. Pearl, Kamp Katrina's main protagonist, who created a tent community for 14 people in her backyard. At other times we stayed in those very tents in her backyard. Moving into the film's location granted us direct entry into the everyday activities of people and their lives within the lived experience and visceral textures of this makeshift environment: sounds, smells, and movements. Immersion in this environment as researchers put us into immediate contact with experiential situations before, during, and after they occurred, and it also led to ethical challenges. As discussed throughout this book, video ethnography avoids verbal exposition and instead explores the experiential rhythms of ethics as part of an empirical narrative. *Kamp Katrina* is no exception and is a good example of the sensuously expansive possibilities of video ethnography. As a video ethnography it reflects ethnographic practices and sensibilities that rely on immersion in the immediacies, and even discomforts, of lived sensory, sonic, and ethical experiences. *Kamp Katrina* premiered at the South by Southwest Film Festival, Austin, Texas (SXSW), and subsequently screened on TV and digital platforms (i.e., Netflix, iTunes, Kanopy) in the US and Canada.

Immediacy and experiential ethics

Immediacy is a phenomenology of the felt, the gestural, and the tactile moment of physical encounter that occurs when video ethnographers situate themselves within experiential encounters. Ripe with flux and contradiction, immediacy is also part of an ethical experience that must be interpreted through what Ferrell (1997, pp. 10–11) describes as *verstehen*:

> a process of subjective interpretation on the part of the social researcher, a degree of sympathetic understanding between researcher and subjects of study, whereby the researcher comes in part to share in the situated meanings and experiences of those under scrutiny – its moments of pleasure and pain, its emergent logic and excitement – within the larger process of research.

Video ethnography draws on the sensory experiences of immediacy from an embedded, embodied position, likewise treating ethical circumstances and situations with the same embodied immediacy that stems from sharing or participating in the world of filmed subjects during filmmaking. Ethical experiences or dilemmas in which boundaries are tested or must be negotiated, are an inherent part of the live, social experience of filmmaking. While prose is able to communicate ethical features, video ethnography is inherently immediate so that viewers immersively and sensuously experience the suddenness and murkiness with which ethically challenging moments can unexpectedly arise. This visceral approach and capacity changes audiences' relationship to ethical dilemmas in important ways that surpass written studies.

The sensory aesthetics of experiential ethics that *interpretively craft* video ethnography is groundbreaking for research, not least because the rise of video ethnography ushers in terms of video ethnography's reliance on building intimate relationships with subjects, sharing in their world, and opening up subjects' ethically ambiguous situations through which an audience

> can begin in part to feel and understand the situated logic and emotion of crime. It means that [video ethnographers], as far as possible within the limits of personal responsibility and professional identity, must be there in the criminal moment ... if they are to apprehend the terrors and pleasures of criminality. It means that [video ethnographers] must venture inside the immediacy of crime.
>
> *Ferrell 1997, p.11*

Video ethnography values proximity to lived immediacy and fully acknowledges and works with the flux of ethics, over the objectivity or authoritarianism of a more distant, fixed set of rules of ethics. Video ethnographies require that the filmmaker attune to sensory details and ambiguity while in the field through physical proximity to all experiences unfolding in all their overwhelming complexity and ethical dimension: whether they spell joy or repulsion. Ethics arising out of the situation of filming also have an embodied and material dimension, reflecting the researcher's choices and aesthetic decisions and skills – where to place the camera, how to move in response to a changing event, when to remain still, and how to record while maintaining awareness of multiple viewpoints and the surrounding conditions – all of which must be woven into the experiential moments. Video ethnography prizes these skills, and values what the complexity of such unexpected moments can teach. Drawing on *Kamp Katrina*, I offer concrete examples that can be viewed and analyzed through the following links and discussion.

Scene 1: Tammy and Doug (https://vimeo.com/115533207)

The clip above opens up a rich seam of discussion regarding the depth of experiential ethics encountered in the making of *Kamp Katrina*. Discussing the clip in print loses all kinds of sensuous details: tone of voice, crackling flames, food slopped from a metal pan as people sit in chairs surrounding a warm fire pit. The clip palpably evokes the feeling of sitting around a campfire as darkness envelops everyone and strangers open up to one another. A woman named Kelley stands as others sit in chairs around a fire. A man's voice says,

> "Show them that pregnant belly."
> Kelley responds, "I did."
> Tammy, a woman seated, says, "Oh, the baby."
> Kelley leaves the frame of the shot.
> Still sitting in her chair, framed by her husband, Mike, and Kelley's husband, Doug, Tammy drinks beer from a can and looks at Doug and says,
> "All I gotta do is say, 'Watch this for me.'"

Tammy removes her glass eye and hands it to Doug, sitting next to her. The
simmering fire cracks and pops as Doug laughs hard.

"Hold that thought," Tammy says, referring to her glass eyeball.

"Let me get a closer look," Doug responds as he returns the glass eyeball to
Tammy.

Tammy takes her glass eyeball and places it in her mouth to clean it.

"Why you lick it before you touch it?" Doug asks.

Tammy says, "Well because, you know what it is? It's *my* eye and I would
rather touch it, it's me. It's not somebody else's shit. You know what I'm
saying."

Tammy's husband, Mike, continues to cough and spit in the background as
Tammy talks to Doug.

Doug enquires, "Oh, so you spit on that motherfucker?"

"Yea and put it back in my socket," Tammy explains.

Doug, at a loss for words, simply remarks, "Cool."

A moment of silence follows in the darkness. Tammy, with intensity, asks
Doug for permission to speak of her experience directly:

"Can I tell you what happened to me?"

Tammy pauses. She looks around to make sure people are listening, and then
reveals her story of violence.

"A guy beat and raped me. And I lost my eye. My face has been recon-
structed. In my own home."

Doug asks, "How old was you?"

"It was in 2001," Tammy remarks.

Doug responds, "Oh so just like five years ago."

Tammy corrects Doug, "Four years ago."

"My god."

"All this is metal, every bit of this," Tammy remarks as she touches her face.

"Yah I could ..."

"I got a big old gap in my head."

As an audience we feel close to Tammy and to Doug, sharing Doug's listening
space and Tammy's telling space, as the horror of her experience is related,
through the physical object that is her eye, through her understatement, and her
restraint. There is no signposting but Tammy has already said that the attack happened in her own home. Doug doesn't ask any further questions. Tammy's husband Mike consistently coughs in the background. Nothing is omitted or
sanitized and Mike's verbal silence hangs heavily, a possible clue to the perpetrator
of Tammy's physical (and, we extrapolate, emotional and mental) trauma. The
combination of elements supports Back's (2013, pp. 31–32) contention that
"audio recording offers the possibility to tune into the voices in the foreground
but also listen to what [is] contained in the background soundscape." Mike's background coughing and spitting occurs within the inversion of the scene's foreground: Mike's repellent spitting or expectoration (in the UK called "gobbing,"
in the US known as spitting a loogie) is grossly corporeal. Generally researchers

tend to sanitize, or omit altogether, moments that are repellent, for fear of alienating audiences as indicated above by Becker (1999). In *Kamp Katrina*, the inclusion of these vile or base moments helps the film to retain sonic textures, spatial immediacy, and the aesthetics of experiential ethics; they become part of a larger investment into a mediated immersion of the empirical and experiential moment.

Unlike the written form, such events can occur simultaneously so that experiential ethics reflect the researcher's actual presence within the circumstance being evoked. Such an approach collapses experiential distance and requires the cultivation of trust and intimate contact. In other words, Mike needed to feel comfortable enough with the filmmaker to openly spit and Tammy needed to feel uninhibited enough with the filmmaker's presence to tell her story and to remove her glass eye. In a sense, video ethnography finds ethical expression within the *craft of the film itself* because it involves being there, in the moment, and witnessing, or letting unfold, raw, unedited, and complex ethical material that involves small details of timing, surprise, and transgression. Digital technologies allow ethnographers to bring real-life atmosphere, situational physicality, and flux into a moment in which issues of violence, crime, harm, and ethics arise, as in the example of Tammy showing the impact on her body of a beating.

> These perspectives further emphasize that methodologies inevitably intertwine with theoretical stances, political choices, and the social situations in which they are practiced. Because of this intertwining … field researchers cannot conveniently distance themselves from their subjects of study, or from the legally uncertain situations in which the subjects may reside, in order to construct safe and "objective" studies.
>
> *Ferrell 1997, p. 8*

The proximity of close encounters of this kind involves an ethics of being embedded in the moment, however raw or compromising, rather than adopting the more traditional generalized "hands-off," or "do no harm" approach that written codes of ethics and conventional research instructions tend to favor. The outcome is something messy but true, more like a literary or dramatic moment than a piece of dry, extrapolated research, but more fully inflected with the physical presence, atmosphere, nuances, cadences, and ironies of real-life utterance and situation than any written description could depict.

Media immersion into experiential ethics

If immediacy is the moment of tactile, present encounter between video ethnographer and all experiential ethics arising within a shared, lived space, then media immersion is the practice of sonically and visually sharing these tactile encounters in which slippery moments of ethics are aesthetically experienced. This practice of media immersion that video ethnography makes possible is precisely what Ferrell suggested almost 20 years ago when he argued for an experiential methodology to unravel the lived meanings of ethics (Ferrell 1997, p. 3). Ten years later after making this argument, Ferrell (2007) clarified his immersive approach by connecting it to *media* and ethnographic filmmaking practices in his analysis of *Kamp Katrina*:

> Over the past decade or so there's emerged among various writers and researchers a new way of understanding the conduct and misconduct of human affairs ... [and] does so through the lens of meaning, emotion, and media ... [video ethnographers] aren't hesitant to acknowledge this mix, though – in fact they often jump in the middle of it.
>
> *Ferrell 2008, p. 3*

Ferrell's notions of "media" and "jumping in the middle of it" are crucial for media immersion into ethical ambiguous terrain and learning how to evoke the circumstance.

As an approach to ethics, media immersion makes two main contributions to video ethnography. First, it allows researchers to record the expressive characteristics of experiential ethics through attuned, phenomenologically-based, embodied attentiveness. Second, when properly attuned to sensory experience, media immersion allows the immediacy of the ethical circumstance to be intuitively anticipated, corporeally felt, and, later, after editing and release, sensuously interpreted by audiences – an experiential outcome that conventional qualitative and quantitative research cannot rival. Hence, this is one reason why and how, according to Marks (2000), the haptics of cinema is felt on the body of the viewer – often in uncomfortable ways. I would also go further to suggest that the experience of ethics has a haptic aspect often overlooked, yet well served by the sensuousness of video ethnography. Video ethnography translates and transmits the immediacy of ethics and ethical situations, by allowing their experiential circumstances to arise organically through scenes that have a strong physical atmosphere and that resonate visually and sonically on the skin of the viewer's body. Audiences feel and experience the ethics rather than perceive them cerebrally or textually. They hear tone of voice, they listen to silences and pauses, and they witness responses and reactions, including gestures and silences, or even spitting, as layers – foreground and background, occurring simultaneously.

Scene 2: domestic abuse (https://vimeo.com/115533206)

The second clip, included for consideration of immediacy and the capacity for video ethnography to bring audiences into close proximity with ethically uncomfortable situations, opens with a couple inside a messy room, exchanging words that betray a tone of harried aggression, culminating in a moment of verbal abuse. After the man exits downstairs, Kelley, a young pregnant woman, mutters partly to herself and partly to the filmmaker about her mental state of longing for her husband's abuse to end, questioning why she should have to put up with it. She drags on a rolled-up cigarette and stares into space pensively. An ellipsis takes the moment into a later point during the night. She scene has already been set by Kelley's fearful words about lying in bed waiting for the sun to come up (which translates to wondering if she'll get through a night without coming to harm at the hands of her husband who has called her "an evil bitch"). Purple skies reflect the ominous tone of emptiness and loneliness. Disembodied sounds intrude into the landscape. The audience hears a woman (Kelley) scream.

> Kelley screams, "Stop! Then stop."
> Doug responds with a whisper, "Shut your fucking mouth."
> Kelley shouts, "Why are you punching me!"

The audience hears Kelley's visceral screams and articulated pain – "Ow!" – followed by the sound of a slap inside the darkened room. Kelley frantically runs into frame, screaming, "God damn it. Cause man, I'm sick of you getting drunk!" She pauses, intently stares into the room, and points her finger while exclaiming, "I'm gone man! I've had enough." The detached yet intimate immediacy of the moment is unnerving. Kelley quickly exits the room, enters the abandoned streets, and dictates to the filmmaker her stream of thoughts as she walks through the darkness, searching for a place to sleep. Her pregnancy compounds the ethical problems depicted in this harrowing, intensely physical scene of *Kamp Katrina*.

The camera through is mostly immobile, unflinching, observing immediacy in a way that verges on the detached and voyeuristic, recording the violence without seeming to intervene or show a human or emotional response. The editing techniques omit the interaction between the directors and Kelley, instead opting to fold the audience into the violent relationship in all its uncomfortable sonic and physical detail – an example of experiential ethics. In this way *Kamp Katrina*'s experiential ethics actively connects the audience members to – and implicates them in – the relationships of violence as it unexpectedly erupts. Such an ethical encounter with intimate violence is unnerving, and it forces the audience into an ethical dilemma in which they must evaluate the filmmaker's decisions as well as their own unexpected involvement: what does one do when confronted with such a scene? Does one intervene, observe, continue to film, walk away, call for help … join the domestic violence? Yet the scene's mimetic power reflects the truth of how violence arises unexpectedly, in the middle of night, half dreaded yet complex and difficult to prevent, present within an intimate relationship, yet impossible to curb. The very privacy of the world of the couple allows the violence to take place, and, while the camera is present, the filmmaker honors the wider truth of Kelley's situation, which is that when she is in private with Doug, her husband, she is alone.

The choices and strategies of *Kamp Katrina* honor the immersive experience, however murky, low quality, rough, disjointed, or challenging to follow and synthesize. Jarring, fragmented speech does the opposite of what speech more traditionally does in documentaries: instead of orientating or explaining, speech in this example is raw, panicked, immediate, drawing audiences into participation in the frightening sounds of unfolding domestic violence. Domestic violence becomes a synesthetic experience of aesthetic expressions, through which our empathy for Kelley is heightened because we feel, through the presence of the filmmaker, her lack of clear choices, the complexity of her situation, her inability to find safety and rest in the middle of the night, as a pregnant woman. The microphone, placed within the scene of Doug's abuse, records the sonic and visual immediacy of "being there." The raw sounds of his criminal violence are abrasive, off-putting, horrific; the haunting visuals implicate audience members as mutual participants in the violence. The audience's imaginary is opened up: this kind of violence could be going on anywhere behind walls and closed doors – only the presence of a microphone allows it to be detected. While audiences may refuse to participate by closing their eyes, turning their heads, or leaving the screening, the violence arises so quickly that most audiences will be affected, whether they like it or not, because the sudden moment plays out without setup or warning. This is an example of experiential ethics through which the filmmaker brings the audience into the scene as closely and fully as possible to use all filmmaking tenacity to evoke the messy and uncomfortable details of domestic violence, and to help capture its complex dynamics and some of the reasons it is so challenging to prevent or police.

Unpacking the conditions under which the scene was filmed and the ethical framework for it, will help to illuminate a larger set of ethics, beyond immediacy, or being in the moment with our subjects in *Kamp Katrina*. We recorded the abuse footage shown and heard in this scene after several lengthy discussions with Kelley. Doug's abuse of Kelley had become an almost weekly occurrence, increasing in intensity and severity on a weekly basis. We called the police, but they dismissed the reports as "personal domestic problems." No one else in *Kamp Katrina* intervened. My co-director Ashley and I became frustrated and we asked Kelley how we could help. She asked us to film the abuse as a way to humiliate and hold Doug accountable. After we began to do so, we found that our presence with the camera often dissuaded Doug from hitting Kelley, rather than encouraging it. In this way, the camera itself became a tactic to prevent Doug from attacking Kelley, but it also provided sensory evidence of the crime; the camera functioned as both recorder and deterrent.

Our approach in *Kamp Katrina* is an example of pushing the limits of media immersion through an inevitable muddling of ethical boundaries to illustrate Katz's challenge to "violate the reader's [viewer's] sensibilities … Morally as well as sensually, it is likely that some readers will feel personally victimized by my effort to convey the offender's experience" (Katz 1988, p. vii). Immersive techniques that include ethically problematic situations can elicit disgust, repulsion, and can even be rejected, troubling the conscience and unsettling audiences by experientially placing them inside the scene. In these ways audiences also experience and question their own limits. If domestic violence is uncomfortable to witness, is it possible that greater solidarity or empathy with Kelley is felt through experiencing her misery firsthand, than by relying on a written report or stated account? By enabling audiences to feel the visceral, spatial, and sonic conditions of domestic abuse we, as filmmakers, expose audiences to some of the haptic and emotional aspects of domestic abuse that might otherwise be lacking. By bringing to bear all senses, the scene facilitates empathetic and ethically engaged experience of the impact of the perpetrator's actions and the physical, emotional, and mental consequences for the victim, Kelley. In other words, an ethically compromised situation is enacted in ways that only heighten the sense of ethical urgency and in ways that mobilize strong emotions, a situation more likely to result in some kind of preventative action, if only heightened empathy, awareness, and understanding if encountering a domestic abuse survivor. Ultimately, the scene produces sensory knowledge that contributes to understanding of a crime and its victim.

Such moments of emotional and sensory involvement are expanded by the broader social context of a tent community of people who are under immense strain and who live in close proximity to Doug's abuse yet are compromised by their own proximity and relationship to domestic violence, either as victims or as perpetrators. In this way an entire cultural and social landscape is evoked, of stress, addiction, misogyny, and negative life experience, ultimately producing a far more complex, ambiguous, and messy picture of the ethical context for Kelley's situation as an abused woman in the middle of an environmental crisis, than any written theory can ever fully evoke.

To conclude, I will consider how the use of digital software to thoughtfully assemble and edit the kind of immersive experience of ethics described into a crafted, sensory sonic and visual narrative and how editing choices that are geared to the immersive and immediate, form a core of importance as significant for ethical framework as the filming itself.

Video ethnography as narrative sociology

The "craft-enterprise" techniques of video ethnography serves

> a scholarly and moral commitment to inquire into people's lived experiences. It thus shares an interest in examining the "cultural trail" that individuals leave behind, the transgressions, the flawed decisions, the cultural and personal artifacts and traces of a life lived that help understand human behavior.
>
> *Apsden and Hayward 2015*

In other words, the difficulties of life – transgressions, ethical quandaries, illegal behaviors – are a part of life and of value for knowledge and consideration.

A craft-enterprise approach to video ethnography requires that researchers evoke the ethics of the situation from the raw materials of lived sensory experience into a narrative order or flow – much as a researcher must choose which words to include in a written analysis. As Robert Gardner describes it,

> Film is another way of telling stories. It's a species in the same genus of endeavor as painting, musical composition, photography, or any other mode of expression. As filmmakers, we take up cameras and sound recorders instead of brushes or word processors, and we set about making something that has shape, content, and meaning. The operative word is "make," whether what is at issue is called documentary or narrative, whether it deals with actuality or invention. All filmmaking consists in shaping something in such a way and with such materials and devices that it becomes an object, an object that is always an invention: another item of culture with form and content.
>
> *Gardner 2010, p. 249 cited in Warren 2010*

The ethically fluid complexities and situations haptically witnessed in video ethnography arise from people's lived experiences and the social context surrounding them. I argue that we can arrive at a working framework of experiential ethics as a mediated immersion into circumstances of lived experience that are interpretively recorded, crafted, and depicted into a cinematic narrative.

Crafting ethics into an experiential narrative hones a researcher's empathic sensibilities to interpretively record lived experience and also introduces these complicated moments to audiences who can interpret them. The skills of craft allow a sensory narrative to become interpretable or intelligible for audiences to encounter and experience as an open-ended event that hones their own empathic sensibilities and interpretative capacities. Allowing audiences to experience material in this way takes judgment and skill, and is as skilled, measured, and thoughtful as writing an essay or argument. A final example of how the following scene from *Kamp Katrina* was filmed and edited will allow me to further demonstrate some of the thought and craft that goes into producing substantive experiential ethics on screen.

Scene 3: "I don't want to be a Jane Doe" (https://vimeo.com/ 115533903)

If we consider ethics to be a fundamentally expressive set of ways in which modern society organizes itself and understands how human beings feel, live, and act in the world, rather than a set of rules, then video ethnography's focus on expressive behaviors immerses audiences deeply in human dramas of pain and pleasure and ethical understanding. The setting or backdrop to Kelley's experience of being the victim of domestic abuse is far from a comforting or nurturing landscape. There's no hospital in the area; no food stores; no restaurants, medical centers, or domestic abuse shelters. The neighborhood is a barren, empty, and desolate space, and remains so for Kelley until she encounters David and Ms. Pearl, who provide physical contact, supportive words of guidance, and emotional empathy. Visual images in the background to Kelley's dramatic life story suggest decay and death. The camera is mobile and attuned to scale, sense of place, pace, and the temporal, and all of these factors come together in the narrative to meaningfully inflect Kelley's sensory, sonic, and spatial experience. This fully expressive storytelling style translates the ethical experience of making the film and the circumstances and conditions under which subjects are living into a tangible cinematic experience. The camera moves alongside Kelley, witnessing that both she and her environment are devastated and unraveling under stress and destruction.

The lived experience of the scene I have included for discussion is shot in a way that deliberately includes Kelley's gestures as part of its narrative flow. This attunement – the intimacy between filmmaker, the ethics of the moment, and protagonist – helps to reveal to the audience the physical presence of Kelley as she negotiates the setting in which she lives. Both Kelley and the landscape have endured hardships, and each reflects the other – and these features are bound into the experiential ethics of film. While Kelley comments that she doesn't want to be a "Jane Doe" and die with no one around, her dismal surroundings remind us that death is at the forefront of everyone's mind at such a time of crisis, as thousands of people have just died in the very streets along which she walks, as a result of Katrina's devastation.

Kelley explains,

> See, Doug's [her husband] a chicken shit; he don't want to face people. I'll face people. I'll face Ms. Pearl and I'll tell her every fucking god honest truth about me. You wanna know why? I'll tell you something. I was partying one night [before Hurricane Katrina] and I was doing a bunch of cocaine and I went into seizures. I woke up in a hospital with a wristband that said "Jane Doe" on my wrist. And I wondered what would it be like for someone, you know, to be buried with no family around and nobody knows what happened to them. You know what I mean? I don't want to be a Jane Doe. I don't want to be a Jane Doe. I'm not a Jane Doe.

Kelley's situation of personal distress and abandonment is one that is mediated as a complex sensory experience, in which she is rushing headlong (walking quickly) while verbally thinking out loud and sharing her fears and her process of coming to a realization that something needs to change. Because of the way in which the film is crafted the audience is able to empathically share in Kelley's situation. The camera doesn't passively eavesdrop nor does it pull away. It is present and close. We see and hear Kelley's voice tremble with fear and remorse, hear her cry in agony, witness how she walks in an unstable, rambling state through the ruined landscape as she expresses her longing for compassion, safety, nurturing, and support. This scene is an ethical narrative, crafted to allow audiences to experience and feel Kelley's situation sensuously and affectively, with empathy and understanding. Eventually Kelley makes her way to *Kamp Katrina* and here she opens up about the drugs she has used while pregnant. As she receives advice from Ms. Pearl's husband David, Ms. Pearl shows her own empathic response to Kelley, talking about the added toll on everyone in New Orleans, of the stress of Katrina, the "smell of death," and seeing "one's city all torn up." Ms. Pearl's comments reflect how sensory experience – of smell, taste, atmosphere – is woven into the fabric of an ethical narrative that pays attention and attunes to the physical conditions of life.

Ms. Pearl:

> I guess the reason get drunk more is to try and stop the pain ... We woke up and cried last night. You know, to see your city all torn up and the smell of death ... You go to sleep and the smell of dead bodies and wake up and smell dead bodies. You can't get in the house. You can't run away ... Because they're still out there. They're out there. It's like all those people are still in the attics and on the bridges. They're standing there even though they're gone ... When you drive over the freeways you can still see things when people were there. They haven't even picked the stuff up yet. You could tell people were sleeping there and stuff. Sometimes I think I can't stand it.

In the scene, Kelley's eyes are swollen and red and she is hunched over. She is a picture of despair. Her situation is dire: her husband, Doug, is abusive, she is unemployed, on the verge of becoming an addict, and has no place to sleep other than the streets. With no money, no family, and little social capital to grant her mobility or networks of care to redirect her situation, Kelley turns to the anonymity of abandoned buildings to find comfort. Experiential ethics and a sensory aesthetic evoke the experience of abuse, anonymity, loneliness, and abandonment. In the next scene in the film Kelley is seen in an entirely different part of New Orleans – an uptown hospital. Here, she gives birth to a premature baby addicted to crack cocaine and heroin. Shortly after the production of the documentary ended, Kelley experienced acute liver failure and died.

Conclusion: experiential ethics and the public sphere

The rise of sensory studies has led to increased interest in using audiovisual technologies to access the latent and explicit fabric of lived experience. Video ethnography is now discussed using a theoretical framework, and with reference to methodological practices, and an ethical dimension. However, with the emergence of video ethnography as a methodological practice, it becomes imperative to examine its ethics. Video ethnography presents *crafted media as experiential knowledge* as a means of adding to and expanding the rich tradition of *describing* and *interpreting* media, yet, as I have intimated earlier in this book, little discussion exists of the ethics of video ethnography as a practice, because there is still too little written about the making of video ethnography in general. This chapter has attempted to fill in this gap by discussing aspects of ethical practices within video ethnography.

In my analysis, I have shown how researchers who integrate video ethnography techniques into their existing methodological approaches are able to inflect fleeting traces and nuances of lived experiences over time, and thereafter craft those experiences as sensory scholarship in the form of ethnographic media. Through this practice, the video project is made with methodological acumen and ethnographic sensibility to become a medium for interpretation and analysis, and for emotive, empathic feeling. I have addressed throughout this book how filmmakers evoke lived experiences and craft their matter into visual and aural stories with several case studies. The presentation of lived experiences recorded during the making of video ethnographies can expand and broaden interpretive possibilities of subject matter rather than foreclose its meaning. The open-ended ambiguity of contemporary video ethnographies does not orientate viewers toward a closed system of meaning. Video ethnographies can immerse viewers into "an experience" through the recording of ambiguity and dislocating features of subject matter. Disorientation can actively engage viewers through estrangement by making the familiar unfamiliar and the unfamiliar familiar.

Traditional criteria for textual social sciences include truth, accuracy, and empirical rigor. Inherent in these criteria are epistemological assumptions about notions of reality, objectivity, and truth. Reality, for example, is assumed as something external, out "there" *sui generis* to be discovered, found, and reported. But these criteria overlook aspects of subjectivity such as point of view, lived experiences, sensory immediacy, and the co-creation of multiple realities and multiple truths embedded in layers of culture and material existence as a *relational experience*. I have presented *Video Ethnography* as an in-depth ethical, methodological, and theoretical framework to demonstrate how social scientists can work within several experiential modes to craft short, medium, and long films as a new form of poetic language in the social sciences. Ingold (2015, p. 8) succinctly summarizes such an approach:

> "Enough of words," my muse declared, and I sympathize. We are suffering, in academic life, from a surfeit of words. It would not be so bad if these words, like good food, were rich in flavor, varied in texture, and lingering in the contemplative feelings they evoke. Carefully selected and well-prepared words are conducive to rumination. They enliven the spirit, which responds in kind. But the fact that word-craft of this kind has been hived off to a restricted domain, known as poetry, is indicative of where the problem lies. If writing had not lost its soul, then what need would

we have for poetry? We go there to find what otherwise is lost. Relentlessly bombarded by the formulaic concoctions of academic prose, weighed down with arcane vocabulary, honorific name-calling, and everextending lists of citations, my muse had had enough. So have I. But I would not want to go the whole way, and to give up on words altogether. Words are, indeed, our most precious possessions and should be treated as such, like a casket of sparkling jewels. To hold such a jewel is to hold the world in the palm of your hand. We can correspond with words, as letter-writers used to do, but only if we allow our words to shine. The challenge, then, is to find a different way of writing.

According to Vannini (2014b, pp. 230–240), more-than-representational research such as video ethnography "renders the liveliness of everyday interaction through methodological strategies that animate, rather than deaden, the qualities of the relation among people, objects, organic matter, animals, and their natural and built environments." Indeed, video ethnography operates within a richness of colors, sounds, dynamic movements, and textures and are disseminated as material of experiences *as a new language in the social sciences.* The vitality present in the poetics of video ethnography exceeds written text and spoken explanation; it speaks to the body and highlights the accidental, the unexpected, and the possibility of presenting research as a vital enactment of experiential data by demonstrating and showing off its dynamic characteristics omitted in textual social science.

> Vitalist approaches argue that there is an exceptional quality to life: a certain impetuous ardor possessed by both inanimate and animate beings which makes life unexplainable by deterministic laws of prediction. As a result, non-representational ethnographies are restless, rich with verve and brio, constantly on the move, forever becoming something else, something originally unplanned.
>
> *Vannini 2015a, p. 320*

Whereas video ethnography attempts to plunge viewers directly into the fluid experiences relationally with pre-reflective attention and external expressivity, linguistic exposition attempts to expand on aspects of the documentary unsuitable to include in the film. As sociology came into existence, it was premised on replicating models from the sciences: data collection, testing hypotheses, replicating studies, and eliminating ambiguity, chance, and bias. Video ethnography, however, does not conform to this epistemological and methodological framework and therefore makes visible taken-for-granted epistemologies in the social sciences. The "frames" of social science – its scientific approach to reality, set of expectations, and its built-in assumptions about how to produce certain outcomes within particular ethical and normative discourses do not apply to video ethnography. Video ethnographies, by contrast, produce different types of knowledge within their own assumptions and open-ended boundaries.

Representational and textual methods assume "the real" is stable and therefore can be "captured" to reflect back to viewers/readers the validity and reliability of a mirrored "truth." Those representations are assumed to provide accurate insight into consistent patterns of experience. Experience, by contrast, is sensuously wedged in and rendered as "wild-being"; it assumes the real is in the making, transformative, fluctuating, and porously assembled through connective tissues that enact affect through co-determination. Video ethnography does not represent the real due to the evasiveness of the ever-expansive fleeting experience. Experience is always already becoming something other than what it is. Experience exceeds representation. Several ethical implications emerge for researchers from this practice, as I will now outline below.

First, researchers are no longer limited to theorizing, analyzing, or writing research articles: the development of video ethnography expands researchers' ability to *craft* media that directly evokes what they see, hear, and witness in the field, yoking the strengths of written text to the visceral experience of audiovisual depiction. Visual depiction blurs nuanced ethical boundaries in the social sciences, as described throughout this book, but filmmakers use self-reflexive techniques to show their presence, indicating the complexity and ambiguity of their role in close proximity to subjects. Second, video ethnography draws upon the rich history of textual ethnography to help viewers understand and appreciate lived experience with sensuous immediacy. However, because the events of sensuous immediacy are difficult to predict or anticipate, subjects are often unable to consent in advance and are also often as equally immersed in the experience being filmed as the filmmaker filming it, if not more so. Third, video ethnography provides opportunities for researchers to go beyond the static methods of positivism, rational choice, and standard (quantitative, qualitative, survey-based) research techniques to engage with sensory studies, visual studies, and documentary art form. It is worth noting that in video ethnography it is largely the case that subjects want to be seen and heard.

Through video ethnography's digital tools and software, social science research culture moves inextricably into a 21st century digital culture of moving images and sound as well as still photography and text. Emergent digital technologies provide new opportunities to reimagine theories, methods, ethics, and knowledge more fluidly and dynamically. The ethical challenges faced by video ethnographers are numerous, as presented in this book, but can be fruitfully and fluidly explored, rather than circumvented by outdated and sometimes inapplicable rules.

Video ethnography techniques allow researchers to vividly evoke lived experience, especially sonic, in ways that surpass text-based media, while text continues to hold the advantage of producing eloquent, in-depth explanation and theoretical insight. When used to augment static text, video ethnography reanimates the kinaesthetic (Vannini 2014a) and brings sensory experience to life as vibrant encounters, opening up a host of ethical concerns that further deepen research questions as they lead to a greater appreciation of social complexity.

The methodological techniques I have described in this book enable researchers to extend the current practice of *critiquing* and *interpreting* media to *producing* and *creating* media, a seismic shift for research. Producing video ethnography offers researchers a unique opportunity to appreciate and depict the experiential flux of daily life while folding into their research the unstable ethics and interpretative outcomes as research experiences of value. Cameras facilitate new ways for researchers to see the world as they contribute to a growing archive of lived experience that will inevitably include ethically ambiguous content, troubling images and sounds, and that can provoke unease and bring visceral immediacy to audiences, especially regarding subject matter involving harm, vulnerability, and empathy. In other words, the very vividness of video ethnography helps to bring about a more "raw" experience that opens up researchers and audiences for their work to dimensions that could otherwise remain buried. Aware of the slippery ethics and instability of interpretation after the film's release and circulation, video ethnography seeks to build into its methodology an *ethics of practice*. Through this ethics of practice, ethical considerations are incorporated into the experience of producing a video ethnography to enhance, expand, and complement the narrative of sonic and spatial environments; experiences originating in taste (Howes 2013), touch (Redmon 2015; MacDougall 2006), smell (Henshaw 2013), and perception (Carrabine 2012). Video ethnography crafts image, sound, and atmosphere through an ethical practice that allows for a wider narrative to enhance the nuances of any filmed situation. A major goal of video ethnography is therefore to find a way to *integrate* ethics into the methodological and aesthetic practice of video ethnography; and how best to merge sensory media's methodologies with a continuous practice of ethics.

Reaching a wide popular audience via digital and theatrical platforms (e.g., iTunes, Netflix, documentary distribution companies, film festivals, TV, Vimeo, and more) in the public sphere, video ethnography can connect bodies into sensuous relationship to scholarly research through directly involving viewers in the experience of the film, thereby bringing the viewers into the ethics of the narrative as a complicit participant. As sensory conduits, video ethnographies offer vibrant encounters, working on the skin and flesh of the audience's bodies (Marks 2000). Open-ended ethnographic encounters filmed as unexpected moments often blur the line between methodology and ethics, sometimes enveloping ethical considerations into a compelling narrative. Video ethnography therefore creates the need for a methodological and ethical shift or felt flexibility that attunes the researcher to their responsibility for the video ethnography-making process while allowing them to remain open and exploratory. Researchers must understand how media is crafted, and craft experiential knowledge as part of an ethical practice. Understanding and appreciating the flexibility and potential ambiguity and unexpected turns of events of video ethnography, opens up opportunities for ethnographic media-making to be reinvented as experiential inquiry, as a methodological practice, and as an ethical form of narrative inquiry that is also an aesthetics of practice – all as a way of knowing and as a form of multimodal analysis that has great capacity to touch and open up the public sphere.

From fact to fiction, the real to the reel, analogue to digital, oral to aural, and aesthetics to ethics (Sniadecki 2014), video ethnography constructs a new theoretical, methodological, and ethical approach to evoking lived experience. Video ethnography's mobile approach is methodologically improvisational – able to adapt to fluctuating circumstances, to negotiate dynamic, fast-changing situations, and to convey the fluid vibrancy of the everyday, or its mundanity, with expressive immediacy. Such an approach contrasts directly with traditional, static research methods. Consider, for instance, how researchers are often taught to *plan* and *control* their research methods in constrained and precise ways: subjects are siphoned into delimited, domesticated spaces, asked to fill out surveys, to respond to interviews, to react to images, and to have their thoughts, attitudes, and observations coded.

This approach, while well respected and to a degree highly effective, is sanitized, and divorced from the experiential textures of actual lived experiences in all their sensory richness. The phenomena pursued by video ethnographers are often by their very nature pre-reflective, nonverbal, fast-moving and immediate – not at all suited to quantitative methods or to static qualitative verbal accounts, much less to generalized ethical practices. Stationary methods omit dynamic activities, fail to reflect plentitude and complexity, eliminate sensuous substance, and fail to apprehend or incorporate the fluctuating ethics and mutability of lived experience. To participate and engage with flux requires an agile, adaptable, and mobile (feral) methodological approach that can reinvent itself "on the go" during the research process (Kusenbach 2003; Spinney 2015). Video ethnography, when conducted with ethnographic sensibility and by adhering to a situational ethics sensitive to changing circumstances, offers a mobile approach with which to engage with the most dynamic lived experience.

For all these reasons, it is my belief that video ethnography *re-wilds* the physicality and sensuousness of conducting research by placing researchers in intimate proximity to the focus of interest in their natural environment. Audiovisual recording technology has facilitated the evolution of key methodological and ethical approaches and practices – leading to an intense vibrancy and capacity to generate aesthetic knowledge as a form of experiential encounter; inviting the viewer to understand and engage with knowledge, methods, and ethics haptically and subjectively, and sometimes with simultaneous sensory responses – moving beyond the hierarchical ordering of written words that tend to pare apart visual and aural components. The key benefits of video ethnography to conducting research are (1) video ethnography extends the capacity of the visual and expands it into the sonic realm; (2) video ethnography increases theoretical sophistication, methodological diversity, ethical nuances, and epistemological possibilities, and (3) video ethnography practices an open-ended stance on interpretation that allows for a nuanced, fluid, ethical, and aesthetic outcome, actively involving audiences in the production of meaning and in all interpretation.

To paraphrase Grimshaw and Ravetz (2009), video ethnography has recently emerged in the social sciences as a hotly contested empirical method and practice that moves beyond established conventions. Ten years after their landmark publication, observational cinema in the social sciences is now positioned as an experiential relationship with its location, subjects, and audiences – and itself. Self-reflexivity merges with aesthetics and ethics to inflect an experiential form of inquiry that acknowledges and embraces relations rather than attempts to erase or simply observe them. Video ethnography, in the manner presented in this manuscript, includes relations in the methods, ethics, and practice of making ethnographic videos.

While popular audiences exist for video ethnographies, thinking about the potential for video ethnographies to reach wide audiences also leads me to raise two major concerns or crucial critiques of video ethnography. The first drawback of video ethnography concerns its tendency to rely on longitudinal form and long periods of immersive field production. Not everyone can spend five years making an ethnographic documentary. Longitudinal video ethnographies sometimes gather lived experience over a very expansive course of time. How might researchers overcome this challenge, while also preserving the integrity of their research? Saunders (2012) cites the emergence of digital technology as a disciplinary transformative "practice" for higher education. Practices, according to Saunders (2012, p. 232), are "routine behaviours derived from a personal or collective knowledge base." An ongoing conundrum is how to advance new practices within an increasingly reductive academic infrastructure that measures the "bottom line" of research output in terms of numbers and text as part of an audit culture of efficiency and new managerialism that overextends and degrades academics (Becher and Trowler 2001, p.13; Daniels and Thistlethwaite 2016, p. 115) – also excluding whole tranches of curriculums and disciplines (Saunders 2012, p. 239) – begging the question, just where do researchers who practice video ethnography fit into this neoliberal model? Vannini (2016, p. 12) addresses this issue when he claims,

> In a global, neoliberal academic environment overpreoccupied with research impact and universities' relevance in their communities, eschewing empirical analysis altogether is not something we should wish to encourage anyone to do (and indeed this might very well be a shortcoming of current non-representational work in general: too few are non-representational research studies in relative comparison to the sheer number of conceptual elaborations and theoretical interventions).

Likewise, Daniels and Thistlethwaite (2016, p. 132) suggest the future of researchers will be a bricolage of practices. "Digital media technologies make it easier to create hybrid projects across fields that are typically separate. The future of being a scholar will include more blending of academia, journalism, and documentary filmmaking" (Daniels and Thistlethwaite 2016, p. 133). They argue that there will be a shift toward digital models of communication and modes of digital scholarship that will present scholars with amazing "new opportunities to do their work in ways that matter to wider publics ... Being a scholar in the digitally networked classroom means guiding students to new knowledge and helping them become lifelong learners" (Daniels and Thistlethwaite 2016, p.138). Digital media technologies, *when implemented as a research sensibility*, will allow scholars to depict, disseminate, and reimagine knowledge as sensuous knowledge, expanding beyond the reach of textual scholarship. Participating in and intimately observing fluctuating activities over time as part of making a longitudinal video ethnography allows researchers to explore and depict immediate experience with great fluency and understanding as an open-ended practice and emergent research technique.

A second criticism of video ethnography stems from ideas concerning the commodified aspect of the "knowledge industry." How can a video ethnography artwork be considered of scholarly value when squared with the fact that research films will be sold on iTunes, Netflix, Amazon, and other digital platforms, thereby becoming commodified products? What kind of possibilities as well as limitations might arise out of this conundrum? Is more gained than is lost and is anything really lost at all? The tools of video ethnography and documentary filmmaking are technologies of culture industries that help produce and disseminate popular knowledge in civic society. We, as academics and knowledge producers (in the culture and knowledge industries), occupy nuanced and contradictory positions: we are consumers, we are consumed, and we make consumable goods. Let me be clear: *there is no space of non-commodification in academia.* Books, journal articles, and documentaries are all part of the culture and knowledge industries. Media can be a way of translating complex ideas in everyday life in contradictory ways. Media production demonstrates Cronon's (1995) proposition of humans' construction of and presence in nature.

Vannini (2014a, p. 397) has demonstrated how the growing popularity of documentaries distributed on Netflix, iTunes, and so on can humble and teach researchers a lot about their role in the public sphere and how to reach different popular audiences beyond textual publications. For example, textual-based articles, chapters, and books are commodified products that are distributed and sold on Amazon, iTunes, and so forth – just as are movies. Articles and movies have distribution companies as do academic publications. Movies and academic publications are branded, packaged, and sold as a commodity, both are consumed by consumers, and both generate income for the distributor and publisher – some more so than others. I believe that video ethnography can maintain a seemingly contradictory position: it can be anti-consumerist while also functioning as a commodity that serves to help undo the harm of commodification (Redmon 2015). I believe that the bigger question is how to tap into existing modes of dissemination in order to further make research available – whether it's free on YouTube or purchased on Netflix or iTunes. As Vannini (2014a, p. 412) states, "more than ever before hybrid TV makes it possible – not easy, but at least possible – to reach a wide, diverse, documentary-savvy, and potentially socially conscious audience thirsty for entertaining and intelligent ethnographic content."

A final concern about video ethnography is the ethics of practice as demonstrated in the final two chapters of this book. I have argued that an ethics of practice in video ethnography arises from the experience and is self-reflexive. Problematic situations can be included in the final version of the film since ethics are not static but ongoing throughout the process of making the film, and after it has been presented in the public sphere. Experiential ethics holds the filmmaker accountable in open-ended ways by including the ethics in the film as an aesthetic practice. Discussions of the filmmaking process arise from experiential ethics in that, sometimes, relations between filmmaker and subjects are also included in the film to show the transparent problems and dilemmas of video ethnography as a practice. Experiential ethics and self-reflexivity are evocative: they can evoke powerful emotions, unexpected reactions by audiences, and trigger knowledge embedded in the body. None of these outcomes can be predicted but should be expected. And this is precisely why video ethnography as an ethical procedure cannot be fully delineated: it is unruly. As all researchers know, unruly practices generate unruly outcomes, and one way to mitigate their harm while also harnessing their evocative power is to include the unruliness in the crafting of the film to demonstrate the process and situation in which contention arises. In other words, experiential ethics, I have argued, is emergent in its open-ended practice and its outcome. Images and sounds are unstable and therefore audiences must relate to them with their bodies – ethics included. Ethics, then, is also an expression or expressive relation between filmmaker and subject, subject and audience, the film and audience, and filmmaker and audience.

The formulation further clarifies the unruly ethics of images and sounds and how they are made and remade during each encounter. Ethics are loosely elusive but they can be experientially woven into the film as an act of production. Thus, video ethnographies as acts of production are affective relations that work haptically on viewers' bodies as a source of corporeal and sensorial knowledge. The body responds experientially to ethical conundrums – when included in the film – before affective encounter can be rationally processed, coded, and subjectively understood. Experiential ethics are felt on the body and hence the reasoning to include self-reflexivity in the film. Video ethnography is not purely observational, as I have argued, but an active producer of the very style of images and sounds evoked on the viewers' screen. It is my conclusion that a shared goal of video ethnography is to bring it "out of the rigid disciplinary and methodological debate following its inception by outlining its potential to reach multiple publics and inspire dialogue among audiences beyond the academy" (Taggart and Vannini 2015, pp. 230–240). Video ethnography's feral and unruly tendencies, methodological advantages, and unique practice-based sensibility offer new and exciting ways to advance this goal.

Notes

1 www.innovativeethnographies.net/.
2 www.popularizingresearch.net/introduction.
3 www.popularizingresearch.net/introduction.

REFERENCES

Adler, Patricia. 1993. Wheeling and Dealing. An Ethnography of an Upper-Level Drug Dealing and Smuggling Community. New York: Columbia University Press.

American Sociology Association Code of Ethics. www.asanet.org/sites/default/files/asa_code_of_ethics-june2018.pdf.

Aspden, Kester and Keith Hayward. 2015. "Narrative Criminology and Cultural Criminology: Shared Biographies, Different Lives?" in Presser, Lois and Sveinung Sandberg (Eds.), Narrative Criminology: Understanding Stories of Crime. Alternative Criminology (pp. 235–259). New York: New York University Press. ISBN 978-1-4798-2341-3.

Back, Les. 2013. "Live Sociology: Social Research and Its Futures," in Back, Les and Nirmal Puwar (Eds.), Live Methods (pp. 18–39). Malden: Wiley-Blackwell.

Back, Les and Nirmal Puwar. 2013. "A Manifesto for Live Methods: Provocations and Capacities." The Sociological Review 60 (S1): 6–17.

Barbash, Ilisa and Lucien Taylor. 1997. Cross-Cultural Filmmaking: A Handbook for Making Documentary and Ethnographic Films and Videos. Berkeley: University of California Press.

Barbash, Ilisa and Lucien Taylor, Eds. 2007. The Cinema of Robert Gardner. Oxford: Berg Press.

Barker, Jennifer. 2009. The Tactile Eye. Berkeley: University of California Press.

Baskin, Jeremy. 2015. "Paradigm Dressed as Epoch: The Ideology of the Anthropocene." Environmental Values 24 (1) February: 9–29.

Becher, Tony and Paul Trowler. 2001. Academic Tribes and Territories. Buckingham: Open University Press.

Becker, Howard. 1999. Tricks of the Trade: How to Think about Your Research while You're Doing It. Chicago: University of Chicago Press.

Bennett, Jane. 2009. Vibrant Matter: A Political Ecology of Things. Durham: Duke Press.

Bishop, John and Naomi Bishop. 2013. "Limited to Words: Visual Anthropology from the Visual Anthropology Review Editors." American Anthropologist 115 (1): 132.

Bonneuil, Christophe and Jean-Baptiste Fressoz. 2015. The Shock of the Anthropocene: The Earth, History and Us. London: Verso.

Brisman, Avi and Nigel South. 2013. "A Green-Cultural Criminology: An Exploratory Outline." Crime, Media, Culture 9 (2): 115–135.

Brisman, Avi and Nigel South. 2014. Green Cultural Criminology: Constructions of Environmental Harm, Consumerism, and Resistance to Ecocide. London: Routledge.

British Sociology Association Code of Ethics. www.britsoc.co.uk/media/24310/bsa_statement_of_ethical_practice.pdf.

Brophy, James. 1997. "Carnival and Citizenship." Journal of Social History 102 (12): 873–899.

Buescher, Monika and John Urry. 2009. "Mobile Methods and the Empirical." European Journal of Social Theory 12 (1): 99–116.

Burawoy, Michael. 2000. Global Ethnography: Forces, Connections and Imaginations in a Postmodern World. Berkeley: University of California Press.

Campbell, Elaine. 2012. "Landscapes of Performance: Stalking as Choreography." Environment and Planning D: Society and Space 30 (3): 400–417.

Carrabine, Eamonn. 2012. "Just Images: Aesthetics, Ethics and Visual Criminology." British Journal of Criminology 52 (3): 463–489.

Carrabine, Eamonn. 2014. "Seeing Things: Violence, Voyeurism and the Camera." Theoretical Criminology 18 (2): 134–158.

Chion, Michael. 1994. Audio-Vision: Sound on Screen. New York: Columbia University Press.

Coole, Dianne and Samantha Frost. 2010. New Materialisms: Ontology, Agency, and Politics. Durham: Duke University Press.

Cronon, William. 1995. "The Trouble with Wilderness; Or, Getting Back to the Wrong Nature." www.williamcronon.net/writing/Trouble_with_Wilderness_Main.html.

Cubero, Carlo. 2009. "Audio Visual Evidence and Anthropological Knowledge," in Chua, Liana, Casey High, and Timm Lau (Eds.), How Do We Know? Evidence, Ethnography, and the Making of Anthropological Knowledge (pp. 58–75). Newcastle: Cambridge Scholars Publishing.

Cubero, Carlo. 2015. "Some Double Tasks of Ethnography and Anthropology: Reflections on Audiovisual Ethnography." Social Anthropology 23 (3): 365–373.

Daniels, Jesse and Polly Thistlethwaite. 2016. Being a Scholar in the Digital Era: Transforming Scholarly Practice for the Public Good. Bristol: Policy Press.

Davies, Pamela, Peter Francis, and Tanya Wyatt, Eds. 2014. Invisible Crimes and Social Harms. London: Palgrave.

Dewey, John. 1934. Art as Experience. New York: Penguin Books.

Ferrell, Jeff. 1997. "Criminological Verstehen: Inside the Immediacy of Crime." Justice Quarterly 14 (1): 3–23.

Ferrell, Jeff. 2007. Kamp Katrina Pamplet. New York: Carnivalesque Films.

Ferrell, Jeff. 2008. Crime and Popular Culture: Theory and Method. Warrensburg: Crime and Popular Culture Conference, Keynote Address, University of Central Missouri, October.

Ferrell, Jeff and Mark Hamm, Eds. 1998. Ethnography at the Edge: Crime, Deviance, and Field Research. Boston: Northeastern University Press.

Foucault, Michel. 1988. Power/Knowledge: Selected Interviews and Other Writings, 1972–1977. USA: Random House.

Gans, Herbert. 2010. "Public Ethnography; Ethnography as Public Sociology." Qualitative Sociology 33: 97–104. Published online: 18 December 2009.

Garrett, Bradley. 2011. "Videographic Geographies: Using Digital Video for Geographic Research." Progress in Human Geography 35 (4): 521–541.

Garrett, Bradley and Harriet Hawkins. 2014. "Creative Video Ethnographies: Video Methodologies of Urban Exploration," in Bates, Charlotte (Ed.), Video Methods (pp. 142–164). New York: Routledge.

Goffman, Erving. 1961. Asylums: Essays on the Social Situation of Mental Patients and Other Inmates. New York: Anchor Press.

Goode, Erich. 1999. "Sex with Informants as Deviant Behavior." Deviant Behavior 20: 301–324.

Grimshaw, Anna and Amanda Ravetz. 2009. Observational Cinema: Anthropology, Film, and the Exploration of Social Life. Bloomington: Indiana University Press.

Habermas, Jurgen. 1991. The Structural Transformation of the Public Sphere: An Inquiry into a Category of Bourgeois Society. Cambridge: MIT Press.

Hamilton, Clive, François Gemmene, and Christophe Bonneuil, Eds. 2015. The Anthropocene and the Global Environmental Crisis: Rethinking Modernity in a New Epoch. New York: Routledge.

Harris, Anne. 2016. Video as Method. Oxford: Oxford University Press.

Henshaw, Victoria. 2013. Urban Smellscapes. London: Routledge.

Howes, David. 2013. Ways of Sensing: Understanding the Senses in Society. New York: Routledge.

Ingold, Tim. 2015. "Foreword," in Vannini, Phillip (Ed.), Non-Representational Methodologies: Re-Envisioning Research. New York: Routledge.

Ivakhiv, Adrian. 2013. "An Ecophilosophy of the Moving Image," in Rust, Stephen, Salma Monani, and Sean Cubitt (Eds.), Ecocinema: Theory and Practice. New York: Routledge.

Jackson, John. 1998. Minima Ethnographica. Chicago: University of Chicago Press.

Jefferies, Fiona. 2013. "Documentary Noir in the City of Fear: Feminicide, Impunity and Grassroots Communication in Ciudad Juarez." Crime Media Culture 9 (3): 301–317.

Katz, Jack. 1988. Seductions of Crime. New York: Basic Books.

Kohm, Stephen and Pauline Greenhill. 2013. "'This Is the North, Where We Do What We Want': Popular Green Criminology and 'Little Red Riding Hood' Films," in South, Nigel and Avi Brisman (Eds.), Routledge International Handbook of Green Criminology. London and New York: Routledge.

Kusenbach, Margarethe. 2003. "Street Phenomenology: The Go-Along as Ethnographic Research Tool." Ethnography 4 (3): 455–485.

Lorimer, Hayden. 2005. "Cultural Geography: The Busyness of Being 'More-than- Representational'." Progress in Human Geography 29 (1): 83–94.

Lorimer, Jamie. 2010. "Moving Image Methodologies for More-than-Human Geographies." Cultural Geographies 17 (2): 237–258.

MacDonald, Scott. 2013. American Ethnographic Film and Personal Documentary: The Cambridge Turn. Berkeley: University of California Press.

MacDonald, Scott. 2014. Avant-Doc: Intersections of Documentary and Avant-Garde Cinema. Oxford: Oxford University Press.

MacDougall, David, Ed. 1998. Transcultural Cinema. Princeton: Princeton University Press.

MacDougall, David. 2006. The Corporeal Image. Princeton: Princeton University Press.

MacDougall, David. 2011. "The Visual in Anthropology.," in Banks, Marcus and Howard Morphy (Eds.), Rethinking Visual Anthropology (pp. 276–295). New Haven and London: Yale University Press.

Manning, Erin and Brian Massumi. 2014. Thought in the Act: Passages in the Ecology of Experience. Minneapolis: University of Minnesota Press.

Marks, Laura. 2000. The Skin of the Film: Intercultural Cinema, Embodiment, and the Senses. Durham: Duke University Press.

Merleau-Ponty, Maurice. 1965. The Visible and the Invisible. Evanston: Northwestern University Press.

Merleau-Ponty, Maurice. 2012. Phenomenology of Perception. New York: Routledge Press.

Merriman, Peter. 2014. "Rethinking Mobile Methods." Mobilities 9 (2): 167–187.

Mitchell, Claudia. 2011. Doing Visual Research. Thousand Oaks: Sage.

Pattberg, Phillip and Fariborz Zelli, Eds. 2016. Environmental Politics and Governance in the Anthropocene: Institutions and Legitimacy in a Complex World. New York: Routledge.

Pels, Dick, Kevin Hetherington, and Frederic Vandenberghe. 2002. "The Status of the Object: Performances, Mediations, and Techniques." Theory, Culture & Society 19 (1): 1–21.

Pink, Sarah. 2009. "Walking with Video." Visual Studies 22: 240–252.

Pretty, Jules. 2013. "The Consumption of a Finite Planet: Well-Being, Convergence, Divergence and the Nascent Green Economy." Environmental and Resource Economics 55 (4): 475–499.

Ratner, Megan. 2010. "Once Grazing, Now Gone: Sweetgrass." Film Quarterly 63 (3 (Spring)): 23–27.

Redmon, David. 2015. Beads, Bodies, and Trash. New York: Routledge.

Rose, Gillian. 2007. Visual Methodologies: An Introduction to the Interpretation of Visual Methods. London: Sage.

Ruddiman, William. 2003. "The Anthropogenic Greenhouse Era Began Thousands of Years Ago." Climatic Change 61 (3): 261–293.

Rust, Stephen, Salma Monani, and Sean Cubitt, Eds. 2013. Ecocinema Theory and Practice. New York: Routledge.

Saunders, Murray. 2012. "Transformations from Without and Within the Disciplines," in Trowler, Paul, Murray Saunders, and Veronica Bamber (Eds.), Tribes and Territories in the 21st Century: Rethinking the Significance of Disciplines in Higher Education. New York: Routledge.

Simpson, Paul. 2011. "'So, as You Can See …': Some Reflections on the Utility of Video Methodologies in the Study of Embodied Practices." Area 43 (3): 343–352.

Sniadecki, J.P. 2014. "Chaiqian/Demolition: Reflections on Media Practice." Visual Anthropology Review 30: 23–37.

Sobchack, Vivian. 1992. The Address of the Eye. Princeton: Princeton University Press.

Spinney, Justin. 2015. "Close Encounters? Mobile Methods, (Post)Phenomenology, and Affect." Cultural Geographies 22 (2): 231–246.

Springgay, Stephanie, Rita L. Irwin, and Sylvia Wilson Kind. (2005). "A/R/Tography as Living Inquiry through Art and Text." Qualitative Inquiry 11 (6): 897–912.

Steffen, Will, Jacques Grinevald, Paul Crutzen, and John McNeil. 2011. "The Anthropocene: Conceptual and Historical Perspectives." Philosophical Transactions of the Royal Society A 369 (13 March): 842–867.

Stoller, Paul. 1997. Sensuous Scholarship. Philadelphia: Pennsylvania University Press.

Taggart, Jonathan and Phillip Vannini. 2015. "Life Off-Grid: Considerations for a Multi-Sited, Public Ethnographic Film," in Bates, Charlotte (Ed.), Video Methods (pp. 230–240, Vol. 2014). New York: Routledge.

Taussig, Michael. 1993. Mimesis and Alterity: A Particular History of the Senses. New York: Routledge.

Taylor, Lucien. 1994. Visualizing Theory: Selected Essays from V.A.R., 1990-1994. New York: Routledge.

Taylor, Lucien. 1996. "Iconophobia: How Anthropology Lost It at the Movies." Transition 6 (1): 64–88.

Taylor, Lucien and Ilisa Barbash, Eds. 2007. The Cinema of Robert Gardner. Oxford: Berg Press.

Vannini, Phillip, Ed. 2012. Popularizing Research: Engaging New Genres, Media, and Audiences. 1st edition. New York: Peter Lang Publishing Inc.

Vannini, Phillip. 2014a. "Ethnographic Film and Video on Hybrid Television: Learning from the Content, Style, and Distribution of Popular Ethnographic Documentaries." Journal of Contemporary Ethnography 44 (4): 391–416.

Vannini, Phillip. 2014b. "Video Methods beyond Representation: Experimenting with Multimodal, Sensuous, Affective Intensities in the 21st Century," in Bates, Charlotte (Ed.), Video Methods (pp. 230–240). New York: Routledge.

Vannini, Phillip, Ed. 2015a. Non-Representational Methodologies: Re-Envisioning Research. New York: Routledge.

Vannini, Phillip. 2015b. "Non-Representational Ethnography: New Ways of Animating Lifeworlds." Cultural Geographies 22 (2): 317–327.

Vannini, Phillip. 2016. http://ferrytales.innovativeethnographies.net/sites/default/files/Non-Representational%20Theory%20and%20Ethnographic%20Research.pdf

Vannini, Phillip. 2017. "Low and Slow: Notes on the Production and Distribution of a Mobile Video Ethnography." Mobilities 12 (1): 155–166.

Vaughan, Dai. 1999. For Documentary: Twelve Essays by Dai Vaughan. Berkeley: University of California Press.

Warren, Charles, Ed. 2010. Just Representations: Robert Gardner. Boston: Studio7Arts and Peabody Museum Press.

Wood, Martin and Sally Brown. 2009. Lines of Flight: Everyday Resistance along England's Backbone. The York Management School, University of York, The York Management School Working Papers.

INDEX

Notes are indicated by "n" followed by the note number.